Sierra Flower Finder

a guide to Sierra Nevada wildflowers

by Glenn Keator, Ph.D.
illustrated by Valerie R. Winemiller

to use this book

- Find some typical leaves and flowers. It may help to look at fading flowers with developing fruits. Also note how the plant grows.

- turn to page 7, make the first choice and go on from there.

The introductory pages explain some terms you'll need and the distribution, habitat and life-zone symbols used.

This book will help you identify non-woody flowering plants (wildflowers) found in the Sierra Nevada mountain range above the foothills which end at about 4,000 feet elevation. For practical purposes, several very rare and endangered plants are excluded.

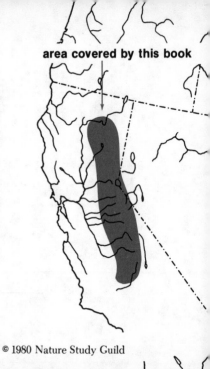

area covered by this book

© 1980 Nature Study Guild

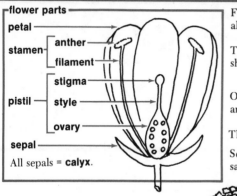

flower parts

petal

stamen ─ anther, filament

pistil ─ stigma, style, ovary

sepal

All sepals = **calyx**.

Flowers having all petals alike are called **regular**.

Those with petals of different shapes and sizes are **irregular**.

Ovaries above petals and sepals are **superior**.

Those below are **inferior**.

Some flowers have a slender, saclike projection called a **spur**.

Flowers may grow in a compact **head**

...along a stem, without stalks, in a **spike**

...on separate stalks in a **raceme**

...in a compound raceme or **panicle**

...in a cluster with stems arising from one point called an **umbel**.

Most leaves have a **blade** and a **petiole**.

Leaves may be **simple** (all in one piece with a bud at the petiole's base)...

...or **compound** (divided into **leaflets** with a bud at the base of the whole leaf).

Leaf-like structures at the base of a flower or group of flowers are called **bracts**.

...or if they're paired at the base of a leaf, they're called **stipules**.

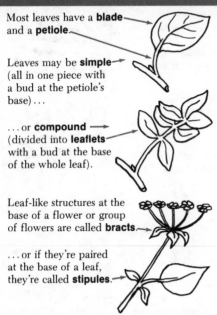

Leaves may be

...**opposite**

...**alternate**

...**basal**.

Leaves or flowers may be **whorled**.

Leaf or petal edges may be

...**entire**
...**lobed**
...**toothed**.

The leaflets or the lobes of a leaf may be arranged

...**palmately**
...**pinnately**.

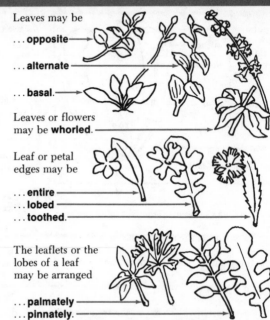

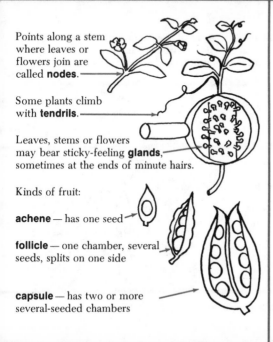

Points along a stem where leaves or flowers join are called **nodes**.

Some plants climb with **tendrils**.

Leaves, stems or flowers may bear sticky-feeling **glands**, sometimes at the ends of minute hairs.

Kinds of fruit:

achene — has one seed

follicle — one chamber, several seeds, splits on one side

capsule — has two or more several-seeded chambers

This symbol shows blooming season.

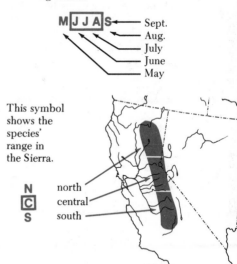

M J J A S ← Sept.
← Aug.
← July
← June
← May

This symbol shows the species' range in the Sierra.

N
C
S

north
central
south

④ These symbols show the life zone where each species is most likely to grow.

SIERRA LIFE ZONES

Alpine Zone — Flowering plants here bloom intensely because spring begins in late July at the very edge of melting snow. Seed set may fail due to short season, so most plants are perennial. Plants form tight, low clumps to conserve water in scanty soils, strong winds, and to be under snow's protection during winter.

Subalpine Zone — The upper edge of this zone has stunted, wind-whipped whitebark and western-white pines, mountain hemlocks. Below are Sierra junipers, lodgepole pines, and the red fir forest. Open areas with good soil have lush meadows, aspen groves.

Montane Zone — The broadest Sierra life zone is marked by vast stands of yellow pines (ponderosa and Jeffrey) with varied mixtures of sugar pine, incense cedar, white fir, black oak, and others. Forests may alternate with broad meadows, or with thick chaparral on rocky or disturbed slopes.

Foothill Zone — This zone, not covered here, is marked by digger pine, blue and valley oak.

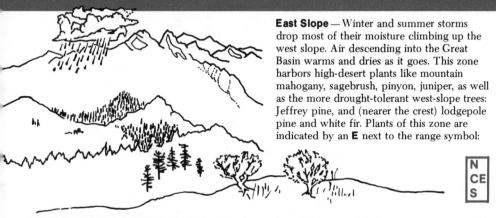

East Slope — Winter and summer storms drop most of their moisture climbing up the west slope. Air descending into the Great Basin warms and dries as it goes. This zone harbors high-desert plants like mountain mahogany, sagebrush, pinyon, juniper, as well as the more drought-tolerant west-slope trees: Jeffrey pine, and (nearer the crest) lodgepole pine and white fir. Plants of this zone are indicated by an **E** next to the range symbol:

Zone Altitudes — It's hard to give exact altitudes for life zones. Zones are at lower altitudes toward the north, higher in the south. Alpine plants, for instance, grow above 11,000 feet on Mount Whitney, at around 8,000 feet in the northern Sierra, and at sea level in the arctic. Zones will be higher on south-facing slopes warmed and dried by extra sun, and lower on cooler north-facing slopes. Basins collect heavy, cold night air, are chillier than adjacent slopes and ridges, and often in a colder life zone. If you want to know what life zone you're in, the kinds of trees present are often the best indicator.

Forest Shade — Plants here often have thin, broad leaves to absorb weak light. Some extract energy from associations with fungi in deep, decaying leaf mold. Plants are most luxuriant in brighter openings and along forest edges.

Rocky, Sandy Soil — Plants here tend to form cushions or sprawling mats, and may have thick, leathery, waxy or hairy, water-conserving leaves — adaptations to coarse soil that retains little water, and to full exposure to wind and sun.

Meadows — Fertile, well watered soil in sunny meadows supports the lushest summer wildflowers. Bee heaven. Species vary from wettest parts to driest. Low spots grade into wetter habitat below.

Streamsides, Swamps, Bogs, Seeps — Spots with superabundant water have soggy or submerged soil which limits oxygen supply to roots and may also become acidic, making nitrogen and other soil nutrients unavailable — conditions which often exclude all but specialized plants.

Disturbed areas — Bulldozers, wheels, trampling feet, fire and grazing make exposed, often compacted soils which are then invaded by alien or weed-like plants, some of which are familiar on farms or in cities.

Chaparral — Old burned areas slowly regenerate the forest, but first a woody-shrub stage appears. Wildflowers are limited to openings in this dense shrub cover.

If the major leaf veins run parallel as in a blade of grass, go to → below

If the vein pattern is net-like or not obvious, go to ⟶ below

 If leaves are arranged in flattened sprays like this go to **Iridaceae**, page 52.

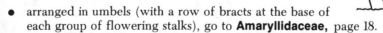

If not, go to

If flowers are irregular, go to **Orchidaceae**, page 76.

If they're regular, and:

- arranged in umbels (with a row of bracts at the base of each group of flowering stalks), go to **Amaryllidaceae,** page 18.

- arranged in racemes, panicles, or solitary, go to **Liliaceae**, page 63.

 If many stemless small flowers are crowded together into what looks like a single flower, go to **Compositae**, page 26.

If not, go to ⟶ next page

(8)

If flowers lack colored petals or sepals, go to **Ranunculaceae,** page 93.

If colored petals or sepals are present, and:

- all of them are separate, not joined, go to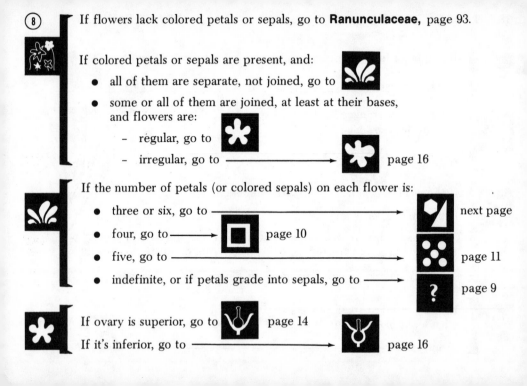

- some or all of them are joined, at least at their bases, and flowers are:

  - regular, go to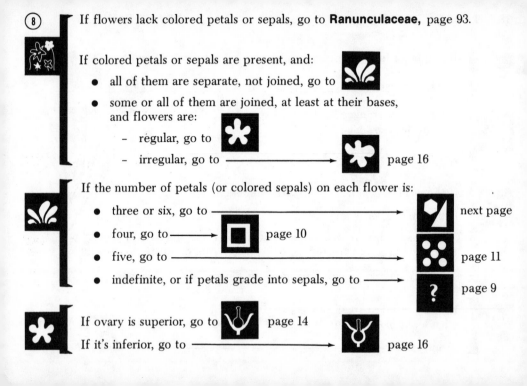

  - irregular, go to ⟶ page 16

If the number of petals (or colored sepals) on each flower is:

- three or six, go to ⟶ next page

- four, go to ⟶ page 10

- five, go to ⟶ page 11

- indefinite, or if petals grade into sepals, go to ⟶ page 9

If ovary is superior, go to page 14

If it's inferior, go to ⟶ page 16

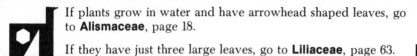

If plants grow in water and have arrowhead shaped leaves, go to **Alismaceae**, page 18.

(9)

If they have just three large leaves, go to **Liliaceae**, page 63.

If they're not as above, go to ———————————→

If the vein pattern on the leaves is net-like, go to ———→

If the vein pattern is hard to see, or if the main veins run parallel to each other, go to ———————————→   page 7

If there are:

- spines, go to **Papaveraceae**, page 78.

- long, spidery, maroon sepals, go to **Aristolochiaceae**, page 20.

- three-sided fruits containing a single seed, go to **Polygonaceae**, page 84.

If petals are red-maroon, go to **Paeoniaceae**, page 78.

If petals are yellow, plants grow in water with floating leaves, go to **Nymphaeaceae**, page 72.

If many small flowers form a dense head like a single flower, go to **Compositae**, page 26.

(10) If flowers have more than ten stamens, go to

If they have fewer stamens, go to

 If sepals fall as flower opens, and there is one compound pistil, go to **Papaveraceae**, page 78.

If sepals stay on flower, and there are several separate pistils, go to **Ranunculaceae**, page 93.

 If flowers are in dense, matted clusters, go to **Portulacaceae,** page 88.

If not, go to

 If each flower has:

- four stamens (superior ovary, turned-back petals), go to **Primulaceae**, page 90.

- six stamens, four long, two short (superior ovary), go to **Cruciferae**, page 41.

- eight stamens (inferior ovary), go to **Onagraceae**, page 72.

- ten stamens (ovary superior to half-inferior), go to **Saxifragaceae**, page 103.

If plants have ordinary leaves, go to ⟶ next page

If they have unusual leaves which are:

- thick, fleshy, succulent, go to ⟶

- modified into insect traps, go to ⟶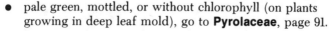

- pale green, mottled, or without chlorophyll (on plants growing in deep leaf mold), go to **Pyrolaceae**, page 91.

If flowers have:

- two sepals, or if pistils are completely fused, go to **Portulacaceae**, page 88.

- five sepals, pistils only scarcely fused, go to **Crassulaceae**, page 40.

If leaves are:

- cobra-like with hood and fangs, go to **Sarraceniaceae,** page 102.

- spoon-shaped, covered with sticky hairs, go to **Droseraceae**, page 46.

- finely divided, bearing dark bladders under water, go to **Lentibulariaceae**, page 62.

(12)

If flowers have ten or fewer stamens, go to **987 654**

If they have more stamens, and ovary is:

- inferior, go to **Loasaceae**, page 70.

- superior, go to — → 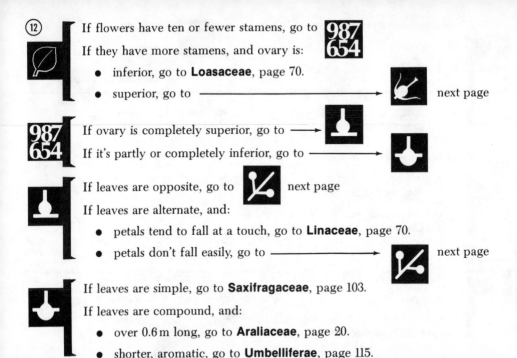 next page

987 654

If ovary is completely superior, go to — →

If it's partly or completely inferior, go to — →

If leaves are opposite, go to next page

If leaves are alternate, and:

- petals tend to fall at a touch, go to **Linaceae**, page 70.

- petals don't fall easily, go to — → next page

If leaves are simple, go to **Saxifragaceae**, page 103.

If leaves are compound, and:

- over 0.6 m long, go to **Araliaceae**, page 20.

- shorter, aromatic, go to **Umbelliferae**, page 115.

If there are two sepals, go to **Portulacaceae**, page 88.

If there are more sepals, go to **Caryophyllaceae**, page 24.

 If styles lengthen into a beak-like structure as ovary ripens, and leaves have green stipules, go to **Geraniaceae**, page 48.

If style and stigma resemble an umbrella handle, go to **Pyrolaceae**, page 91.

If styles are not as above, and:

- leaves have papery stipules, go to **Polygonaceae**, page 84.

- leaves lack stipules, go to **Saxifragaceae**, page 103.

If stamens are fused together into a hollow tube, go to **Malvaceae**, page 71.

If not, go to ⟶

 If leaves have:

- stipules at the base; floral bracts are present, go to **Rosaceae**, page 98.

- black dots (glands, use hand lens); stamens in bunches, go to **Hypericaceae**, page 52.

- neither of the above features, go to **Ranunculaceae,** page 93.

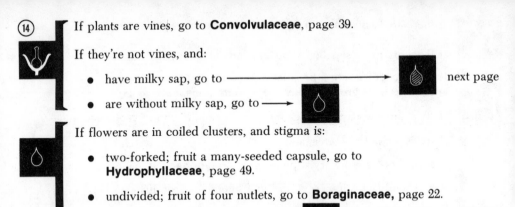

If plants are vines, go to **Convolvulaceae**, page 39.

If they're not vines, and:

- have milky sap, go to ⟶ next page

- are without milky sap, go to ⟶

If flowers are in coiled clusters, and stigma is:

- two-forked; fruit a many-seeded capsule, go to **Hydrophyllaceae**, page 49.

- undivided; fruit of four nutlets, go to **Boraginaceae,** page 22.

If flowers are not in coiled clusters, go to

If plants lack chlorophyll, go to **Pyrolaceae**, page 91.

If plants are green, and:

- stigma is three-lobed, or plants smell skunky, go to **Polemoniaceae**, page 79.

- stigma is otherwise, go to ⟶ next page

If flowers have hoods around center, go to **Asclepiadaceae,** page 21.

If flowers lack hoods, and leaves are:

- arrowhead-shaped, go to **Convolvulaceae**, page 39.
- some other shape, go to **Apocynaceae**, page 20.

If petals spread wide, go to ─────────────→

If they converge into a bowl- or saucer-shaped corolla, and plants are:

- woody at base, go to **Ericaceae**, page 45.
- not woody, and leaves are:
  - basal, go to **Hydrophyllaceae**, page 49. (Also see Pyrolaceae, p. 91, if stigma and style look like an umbrella handle.)
  - along stem, opposite, go to **Gentianaceae**, page 47.

If leaves are alternate, and flowers are:

- blue-purple, go to **Solanaceae**, page 114.
- yellow, go to **Scrophulariaceae**, page 106.

If leaves are opposite or whorled, and flowers are:

- pinkish to red, go to **Primulaceae**, page 90.
- greenish, white and fringed, or purple, go to **Gentianaceae**, page 47.

If leaves are opposite, and flowers are tightly clustered, go to **Valerianaceae**, page 119.

If leaves are opposite or whorled, but flowers are not tightly clustered, go to **Rubiaceae**, page 102.

If leaves are alternate, go to ———————————→

If leaves are compound, go to ———————————→

If they're simple, go to **Campanulaceae**, page 23.

If leaves are over 0.6 m long, go to **Araliaceae**, page 20.

If they're shorter, go to **Umbelliferae**, page 115.

If all petals are fused to form a tube or sac, go to ————→ next page

If only some petals are fused, and others are separate, go to

If the number of stamens is:

- four or six; leaves fern-like, go to **Fumariaceae**, page 46.
- ten; flowers pea-like, go to **Leguminosae**, page 57.
- more than ten, go to **Ranunculaceae**, page 93.

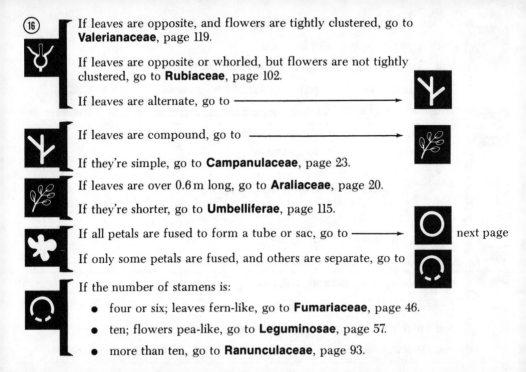

If ovary is inferior, go to **Valerianaceae**, page 119.

If ovary is superior, and:

- plant lacks chlorophyll, go to **Orobanchaceae**, page 77.
- plant lives in water; leaves submerged, go to **Lentibulariaceae**, page 62.
- plant is unlike the above, go to ⟶

If the top of the flower has two separate petals like this with lines marking the lower petal, go to **Violaceae**, page 120.

If a single petal or a fused pair of petals is centered at the top like this ⟶

or this ⟶

go to

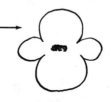

If leaves have an odor when crushed; fruit is of four nutlets, go to **Labiatae**, page 54.

If leaves lack aroma; fruit a many-seeded capsule, go to **Scrophulariaceae**, page 106.

(18) **Alismaceae** (Arrowhead Family) Mostly aquatic herbs, often with tuberous roots. Leaves are divided into petiole and blade. Flowers have three separate sepals and petals, several (sometimes numerous) stamens, and separate, simple pistils.

One Sierra species: **Arrowhead, Tule Potato** ⟶
Sagittaria latifolia

Amaryllidaceae (Amaryllis Family) Grow from fleshy underground tubers, corms, or bulbs. Flowers in umbels with bracts below each umbel. Three sepals, three petals look alike. Stamens are six (occasionally three), stigma three-lobed, ovary three-chambered, fruit a capsule.

If plant has onion odor, and:

- leaves are green at flowering,
  it is **Swamp Onion**
  Allium validum

- leaves are dry; plant
  under 15cm high,
  it is **Sierra Onion** ⟶
  A. campanulatum
  Nine other *Allium* species also
  occur.

If plant lacks onion odor, see next page.

white

purple

purple

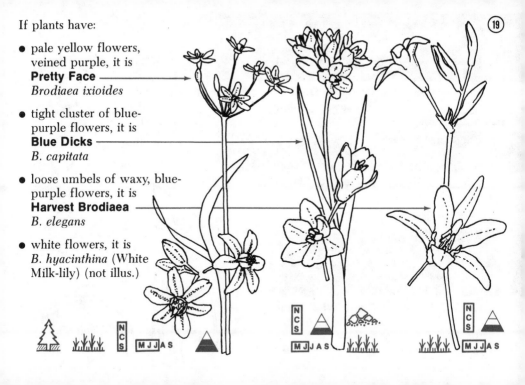

If plants have:

- pale yellow flowers, veined purple, it is **Pretty Face** *Brodiaea ixioides*

- tight cluster of blue-purple flowers, it is **Blue Dicks** *B. capitata*

- loose umbels of waxy, blue-purple flowers, it is **Harvest Brodiaea** *B. elegans*

- white flowers, it is *B. hyacinthina* (White Milk-lily) (not illus.)

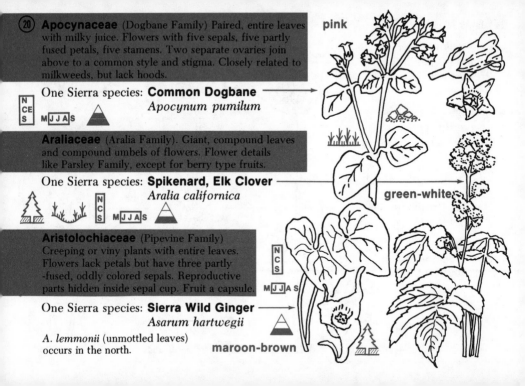

(20) Apocynaceae (Dogbane Family) Paired, entire leaves with milky juice. Flowers with five sepals, five partly fused petals, five stamens. Two separate ovaries join above to a common style and stigma. Closely related to milkweeds, but lack hoods.

One Sierra species: **Common Dogbane**
Apocynum pumilum

Araliaceae (Aralia Family). Giant, compound leaves and compound umbels of flowers. Flower details like Parsley Family, except for berry type fruits.

One Sierra species: **Spikenard, Elk Clover**
Aralia californica

Aristolochiaceae (Pipevine Family) Creeping or viny plants with entire leaves. Flowers lack petals but have three partly -fused, oddly colored sepals. Reproductive parts hidden inside sepal cup. Fruit a capsule.

One Sierra species: **Sierra Wild Ginger**
Asarum hartwegii

A. lemmonii (unmottled leaves) occurs in the north.

pink

green-white

maroon-brown

Asclepiadaceae (Milkweed Family) Leaves are opposite or whorled, have milky juice. Flowers are in loose umbels, have five sepals and petals. Petals are augmented by five hoods (actually, outgrowths of stamen filaments). Two separate, one-chambered ovaries are joined on top by style and five-sided stigma. Stamens are complex, partly fused to side of stigma.

If leaves are:

- hairless, heart-shaped, blue-green, it is **Heart-leaved Milkweed**
  Asclepias cordifolia

- fuzzy, wooly, broad, it is **Showy Milkweed**
  A. speciosa

- narrow, whorled, it is **Whorled Milkweed**
  A. fascicularis

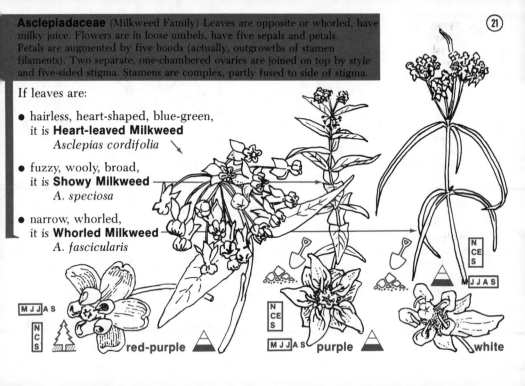

red-purple

purple

white

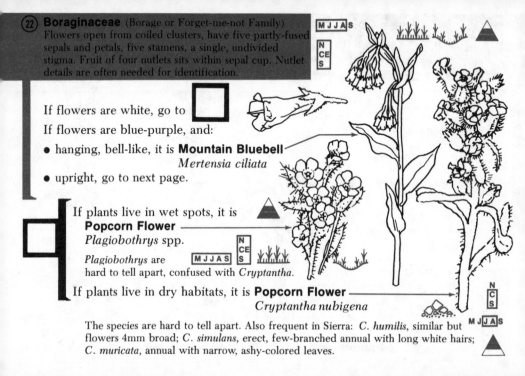

(22) **Boraginaceae** (Borage or Forget-me-not Family)
Flowers open from coiled clusters, have five partly-fused sepals and petals, five stamens, a single, undivided stigma. Fruit of four nutlets sits within sepal cup. Nutlet details are often needed for identification.

MJJAS

NCE

If flowers are white, go to ☐

If flowers are blue-purple, and:

- hanging, bell-like, it is **Mountain Bluebell**
  Mertensia ciliata
- upright, go to next page.

If plants live in wet spots, it is
Popcorn Flower
Plagiobothrys spp.

Plagiobothrys are
hard to tell apart, confused with *Cryptantha*.

MJJAS

NCE

If plants live in dry habitats, it is **Popcorn Flower**
Cryptantha nubigena

NCS

MJJAS

The species are hard to tell apart. Also frequent in Sierra: *C. humilis*, similar but flowers 4mm broad; *C. simulans*, erect, few-branched annual with long white hairs; *C. muricata*, annual with narrow, ashy-colored leaves.

If the nutlets have spreading segments
(look at older, wilted flowers), it is
   Mountain Hound's Tongue
   Cynoglossum occidentale

If fruit segments don't spread, it is
   Stickseed
   Mountain Forget-me-not
   Hackelia jessicae

   Other stickseeds include: *H. nervosa,*
   H. longituba, H. velutina, H. californica, H. mundula.

Campanulaceae (Bellflower Family) Mostly
herbs with simple leaves, milky juice. Flowers
often bell-shaped or tubular with five sepals,
petals, stamens; petals fused. Stigma three-lobed.
Ovary three-chambered. Fruit a capsule.

One Sierra species:

California Harebell
Campanula prenanthoides

blue

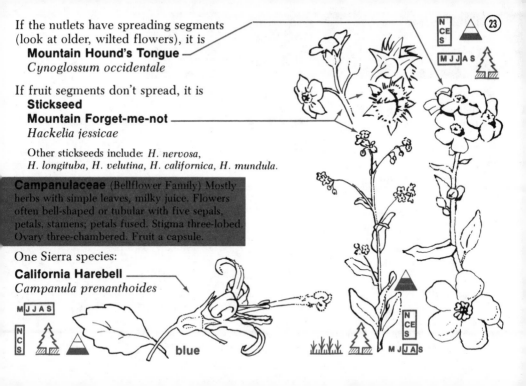

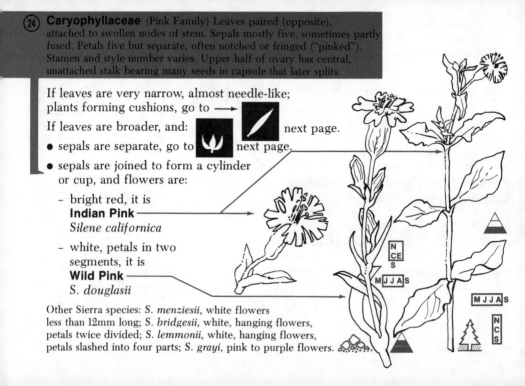

(24) Caryophyllaceae (Pink Family) Leaves paired (opposite), attached to swollen nodes of stem. Sepals mostly five, sometimes partly fused. Petals five but separate, often notched or fringed ("pinked"). Stamen and style number varies. Upper half of ovary has central, unattached stalk bearing many seeds in capsule that later splits.

If leaves are very narrow, almost needle-like; plants forming cushions, go to ⟶

If leaves are broader, and: next page.

- sepals are separate, go to next page.

- sepals are joined to form a cylinder or cup, and flowers are:

  – bright red, it is
  Indian Pink
  Silene californica

  – white, petals in two segments, it is
  Wild Pink
  S. douglasii

Other Sierra species: *S. menziesii*, white flowers less than 12mm long; *S. bridgesii*, white, hanging flowers, petals twice divided; *S. lemmonii*, white, hanging flowers, petals slashed into four parts; *S. grayi*, pink to purple flowers.

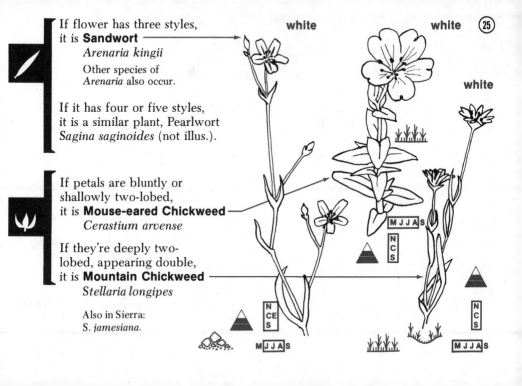

If flower has three styles,
it is **Sandwort** ⟶
Arenaria kingii

Other species of
Arenaria also occur.

If it has four or five styles,
it is a similar plant, Pearlwort
Sagina saginoides (not illus.).

white

white (25)

white

If petals are bluntly or
shallowly two-lobed,
it is **Mouse-eared Chickweed**
Cerastium arvense

If they're deeply two-
lobed, appearing double,
it is **Mountain Chickweed** ⟶
Stellaria longipes

Also in Sierra:
S. jamesiana.

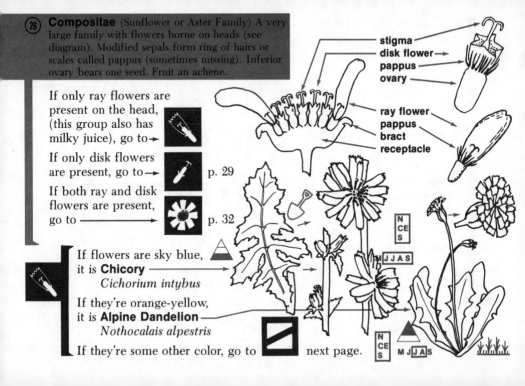

(26) Compositae (Sunflower or Aster Family) A very large family with flowers borne on heads (see diagram). Modified sepals form ring of hairs or scales called pappus (sometimes missing). Inferior ovary bears one seed. Fruit an achene.

stigma
disk flower →
pappus
ovary

ray flower
pappus
bract
receptacle

If only ray flowers are present on the head, (this group also has milky juice), go to →

If only disk flowers are present, go to → p. 29

If both ray and disk flowers are present, go to → p. 32

If flowers are sky blue, it is **Chicory** — *Cichorium intybus*

If they're orange-yellow, it is **Alpine Dandelion** — *Nothocalais alpestris*

If they're some other color, go to next page.

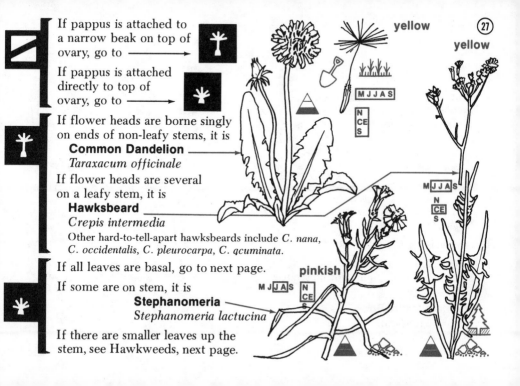

If pappus is attached to a narrow beak on top of ovary, go to ⟶

If pappus is attached directly to top of ovary, go to

yellow ㉗

yellow

If flower heads are borne singly on ends of non-leafy stems, it is
Common Dandelion
Taraxacum officinale

If flower heads are several on a leafy stem, it is
Hawksbeard
Crepis intermedia

Other hard-to-tell-apart hawksbeards include *C. nana*, *C. occidentalis*, *C. pleurocarpa*, *C. acuminata*.

If all leaves are basal, go to next page.

pinkish

If some are on stem, it is
Stephanomeria
Stephanomeria lactucina

If there are smaller leaves up the stem, see Hawkweeds, next page.

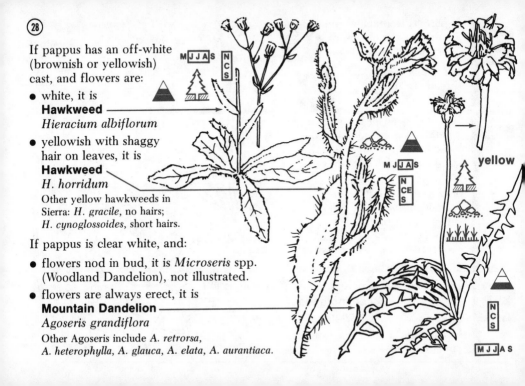

(28)

If pappus has an off-white (brownish or yellowish) cast, and flowers are:

- white, it is **Hawkweed** ———
  Hieracium albiflorum

- yellowish with shaggy hair on leaves, it is **Hawkweed**
  H. horridum

  Other yellow hawkweeds in Sierra: *H. gracile*, no hairs; *H. cynoglossoides*, short hairs.

If pappus is clear white, and:

- flowers nod in bud, it is *Microseris* spp. (Woodland Dandelion), not illustrated.

- flowers are always erect, it is **Mountain Dandelion** ———
  Agoseris grandiflora

  Other Agoseris include *A. retrorsa*, *A. heterophylla*, *A. glauca*, *A. elata*, *A. aurantiaca*.

yellow

If flower heads have wooly hairs on the bracts, and individual flowers are hard to find, go to ⟶ 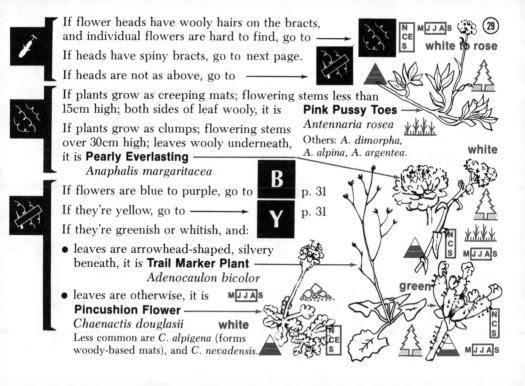 (29)

white to rose

If heads have spiny bracts, go to next page.

If heads are not as above, go to ⟶

If plants grow as creeping mats; flowering stems less than 15cm high; both sides of leaf wooly, it is **Pink Pussy Toes** ⟶

Antennaria rosea

Others: *A. dimorpha, A. alpina, A. argentea.*

If plants grow as clumps; flowering stems over 30cm high; leaves wooly underneath, it is **Pearly Everlasting** ⟶

Anaphalis margaritacea

white

If flowers are blue to purple, go to **B** p. 31

If they're yellow, go to ⟶ **Y** p. 31

If they're greenish or whitish, and:

- leaves are arrowhead-shaped, silvery beneath, it is **Trail Marker Plant** ⟶

  Adenocaulon bicolor

- leaves are otherwise, it is **Pincushion Flower** ⟶

  Chaenactis douglasii   white

  Less common are *C. alpigena* (forms woody-based mats), and *C. nevadensis.*

green

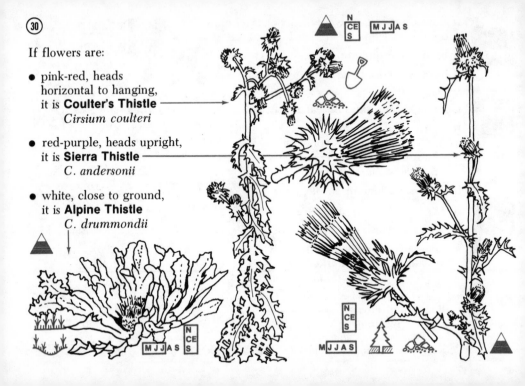

(30)

If flowers are:

- pink-red, heads horizontal to hanging, it is **Coulter's Thistle** *Cirsium coulteri*

- red-purple, heads upright, it is **Sierra Thistle** *C. andersonii*

- white, close to ground, it is **Alpine Thistle** *C. drummondii*

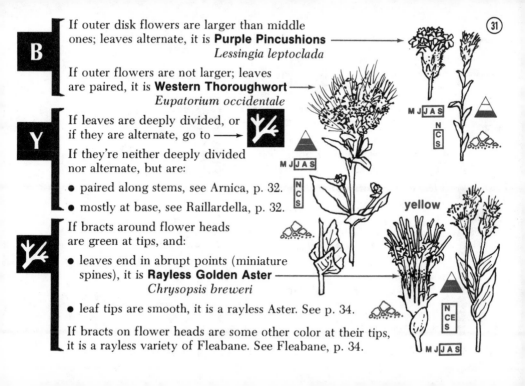

B

If outer disk flowers are larger than middle ones; leaves alternate, it is **Purple Pincushions** —
Lessingia leptoclada

③①

If outer flowers are not larger; leaves are paired, it is **Western Thoroughwort** —
Eupatorium occidentale

Y

If leaves are deeply divided, or if they are alternate, go to —

If they're neither deeply divided nor alternate, but are:

● paired along stems, see Arnica, p. 32.
● mostly at base, see Raillardella, p. 32.

yellow

If bracts around flower heads are green at tips, and:

● leaves end in abrupt points (miniature spines), it is **Rayless Golden Aster** —
Chrysopsis breweri

● leaf tips are smooth, it is a rayless Aster. See p. 34.

If bracts on flower heads are some other color at their tips, it is a rayless variety of Fleabane. See Fleabane, p. 34.

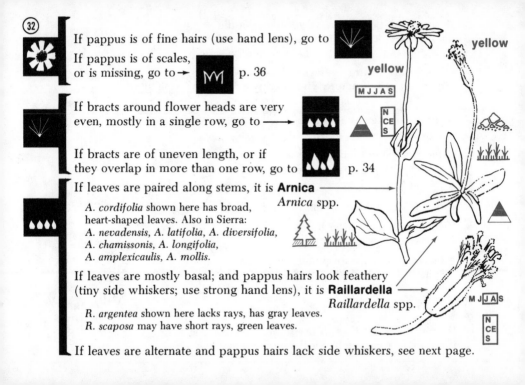

(32)

If pappus is of fine hairs (use hand lens), go to

If pappus is of scales, or is missing, go to → p. 36

If bracts around flower heads are very even, mostly in a single row, go to →

If bracts are of uneven length, or if they overlap in more than one row, go to p. 34

If leaves are paired along stems, it is **Arnica**
Arnica spp.

A. *cordifolia* shown here has broad, heart-shaped leaves. Also in Sierra: A. *nevadensis*, A. *latifolia*, A. *diversifolia*, A. *chamissonis*, A. *longifolia*, A. *amplexicaulis*, A. *mollis*.

If leaves are mostly basal; and pappus hairs look feathery (tiny side whiskers; use strong hand lens), it is **Raillardella**
Raillardella spp.

R. *argentea* shown here lacks rays, has gray leaves.
R. *scaposa* may have short rays, green leaves.

If leaves are alternate and pappus hairs lack side whiskers, see next page.

yellow

yellow

yellow

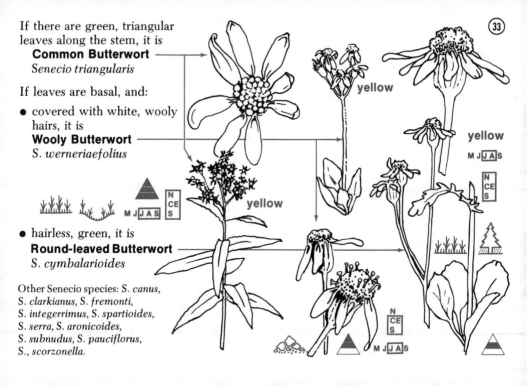

If there are green, triangular leaves along the stem, it is
Common Butterwort
Senecio triangularis

If leaves are basal, and:

- covered with white, wooly hairs, it is
Wooly Butterwort
S. werneriaefolius

- hairless, green, it is
Round-leaved Butterwort
S. cymbalarioides

Other Senecio species: *S. canus,*
S. clarkianus, S. fremonti,
S. integerrimus, S. spartioides,
S. serra, S. aronicoides,
S. subnudus, S. pauciflorus,
S., scorzonella.

yellow

yellow

yellow

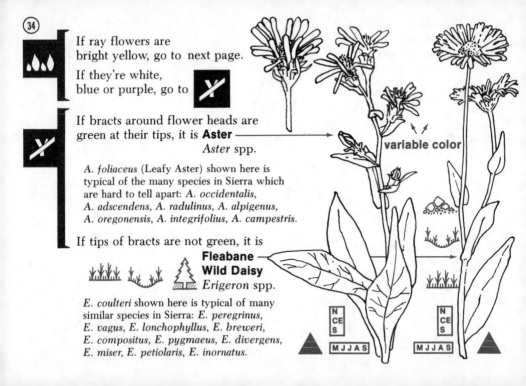

If ray flowers are bright yellow, go to next page.

If they're white, blue or purple, go to

If bracts around flower heads are green at their tips, it is **Aster** — *Aster* spp.

variable color

A. foliaceus (Leafy Aster) shown here is typical of the many species in Sierra which are hard to tell apart: *A. occidentalis*, *A. adscendens*, *A. radulinus*, *A. alpigenus*, *A. oregonensis*, *A. integrifolius*, *A. campestris*.

If tips of bracts are not green, it is

Fleabane
Wild Daisy
Erigeron spp.

E. coulteri shown here is typical of many similar species in Sierra: *E. peregrinus*, *E. vagus*, *E. lonchophyllus*, *E. breweri*, *E. compositus*, *E. pygmaeus*, *E. divergens*, *E. miser*, *E. petiolaris*, *E. inornatus*.

N C E S
M J J A S

N C E S
M J J A S

If flower heads are pea-sized or smaller, in spike-like clusters, it is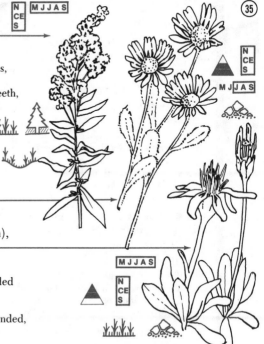

Goldenrod
Solidago spp.

S. *elongata* shown here has hairless leaves, toothed, mostly clustered at plant base. S. *californica* is similar, but leaves lack teeth, have small hairs. S. *multiradiata* has well developed leaves up the stems.

If flower heads are larger, fewer per cluster; and leaves:

● have conspicuous white hairs, it is **Golden Aster**
Chrysopsis villosa

● are not conspicuously hairy (look green), it is **Bush Sunflower**
Haplopappus spp.

H. *acaulis* shown here has densely crowded leaves hiding basal, woody stems. H. *apargioides* lacks wood, grows from taproot. H. *suffruticosus* makes low, mounded, woody subshrubs with narrow leaves.

If ray flowers are yellow, go to

If they're white; foliage ferny, aromatic, it is **Yarrow** —————————
Achillea lanulosa

M J J A S N C E S

If leaves and bracts have sticky glands, it is **Tarweed** —————————
Madia spp.

N C E S M J J A S

M. elegans shown here has showy rays often marked at base with purple. Other common tarweeds are often smaller-flowered, including: *M. bolanderi, M. yosemitana, M. gracilis, M. glomerata, M. minima.*

If disk flowers are borne on a cone-shaped receptacle, it is **Coneflower** —————————
Rudbeckia spp.

R. californica shown here has "cones" over 5cm long. *R. hirta* and *R. occidentalis* have less conspicuous cones.

If leaves and flowers are not as above, go to next page.

M J J A S N C S

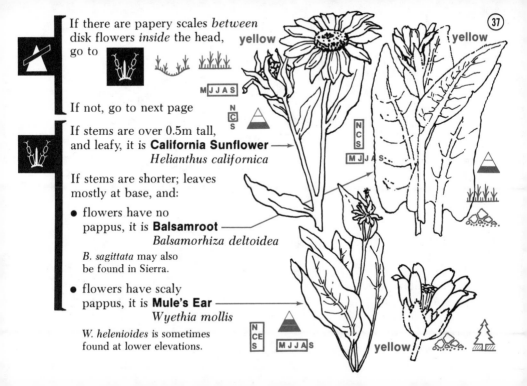

If there are papery scales *between* disk flowers *inside* the head, go to

If not, go to next page

If stems are over 0.5m tall, and leafy, it is **California Sunflower** *Helianthus californica*

yellow

yellow

If stems are shorter; leaves mostly at base, and:

● flowers have no pappus, it is **Balsamroot** *Balsamorhiza deltoidea*

B. sagittata may also be found in Sierra.

● flowers have scaly pappus, it is **Mule's Ear** *Wyethia mollis*

W. helenioides is sometimes found at lower elevations.

yellow

If bracts around flower heads are in one row, it is **Wooly Sunflower** *Eriophyllum lanatum*

If bracts are in more than one row or level, and:

● receptacle is rounded, rays turned down, it is **Sneezeweed** *Helenium* spp.

H. hoopesii shown here has conspicuous rays. *H. bigelovii* has smaller, not obvious rays.

● receptacle is flat, rays spreading, and rays are:

- yellow, it is **Mountain Sunflower** *Hulsea algida*

- purple, it is **Purple Mountain Sunflower** *H. heterochroma* (illustrated next page)

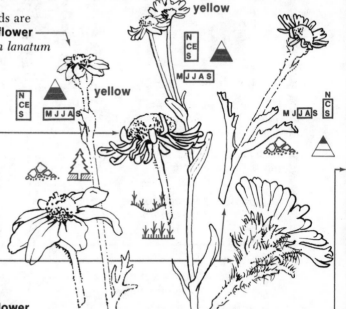

yellow

yellow

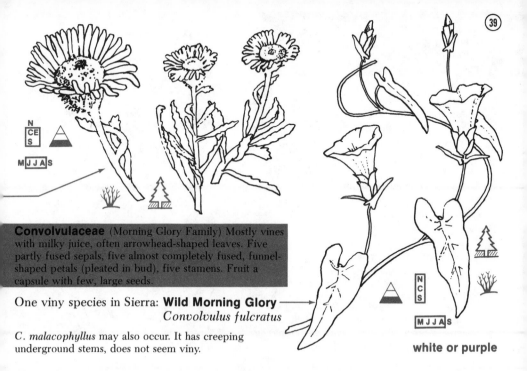

Convolvulaceae (Morning Glory Family) Mostly vines with milky juice, often arrowhead-shaped leaves. Five partly fused sepals, five almost completely fused, funnel-shaped petals (pleated in bud), five stamens. Fruit a capsule with few, large seeds.

One viny species in Sierra: **Wild Morning Glory** *Convolvulus fulcratus*

C. malacophyllus may also occur. It has creeping underground stems, does not seem viny.

white or purple

40 **Crassulaceae** (Live-forever or Orpine Family) Leaves very fleshy (succulent), flowers star-like with five free petals, five or ten stamens, several pistils with ovaries barely fused at bases.

If leaves are very narrow; flowers bright yellow, it is
Alpine Stonecrop ——→
Sedum lanceolatum
S. stenopetalum ssp.
radiatum looks similar
and also occurs.

If leaves are heart-shaped; flowers pale yellow, it is
Broad-leaved Stonecrop ——
S. obtusatum

If stems and flowers are red, it is **Rosecrown**
S. rosea

Other species of this family in Sierra include *S. spathulifolium* (Common Stonecrop) with spoon-shaped leaves, bright yellow flowers; and less common species: *Dudleya cymosa*, tight rosettes of broad, pointed leaves; and *Parvisedum* spp., low annuals with leaves drying up.

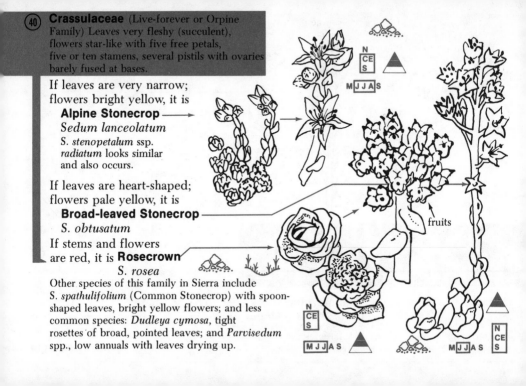

fruits

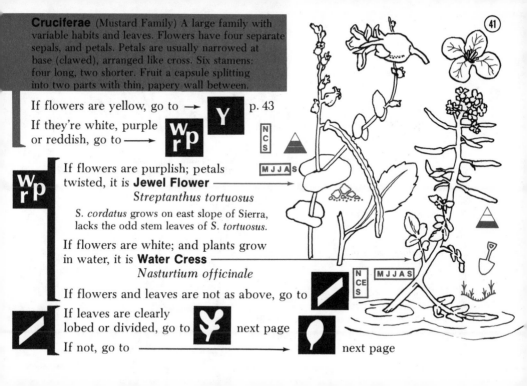

Cruciferae (Mustard Family) A large family with variable habits and leaves. Flowers have four separate sepals, and petals. Petals are usually narrowed at base (clawed), arranged like cross. Six stamens: four long, two shorter. Fruit a capsule splitting into two parts with thin, papery wall between.

If flowers are yellow, go to → **Y** p. 43

If they're white, purple or reddish, go to → **w r p**

If flowers are purplish; petals twisted, it is **Jewel Flower** →
Streptanthus tortuosus

S. *cordatus* grows on east slope of Sierra, lacks the odd stem leaves of S. *tortuosus*.

If flowers are white; and plants grow in water, it is **Water Cress** →
Nasturtium officinale

If flowers and leaves are not as above, go to

If leaves are clearly lobed or divided, go to **Y** next page

If not, go to → next page

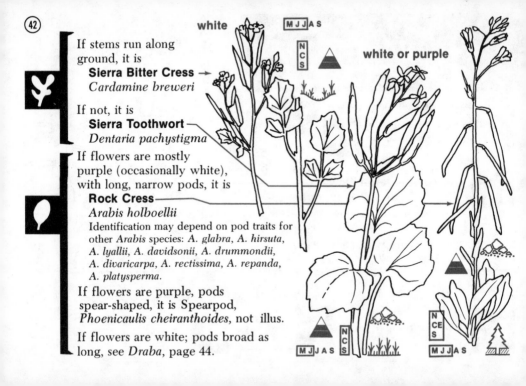

(42)

white

white or purple

If stems run along ground, it is
Sierra Bitter Cress →
Cardamine breweri

If not, it is
Sierra Toothwort
Dentaria pachystigma

If flowers are mostly purple (occasionally white), with long, narrow pods, it is
Rock Cress
Arabis holboellii
Identification may depend on pod traits for other *Arabis* species: *A. glabra, A. hirsuta, A. lyallii, A. davidsonii, A. drummondii, A. divaricarpa, A. rectissima, A. repanda, A. platysperma.*

If flowers are purple, pods spear-shaped, it is Spearpod, *Phoenicaulis cheiranthoides*, not illus.

If flowers are white; pods broad as long, see *Draba*, page 44.

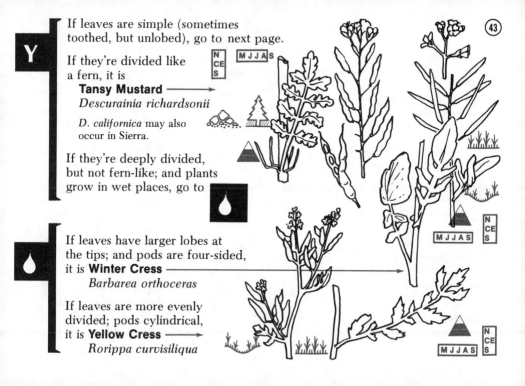

Y

If leaves are simple (sometimes toothed, but unlobed), go to next page.

If they're divided like a fern, it is
Tansy Mustard
Descurainia richardsonii

D. californica may also occur in Sierra.

If they're deeply divided, but not fern-like; and plants grow in wet places, go to

If leaves have larger lobes at the tips; and pods are four-sided, it is **Winter Cress**
Barbarea orthoceras

If leaves are more evenly divided; pods cylindrical, it is **Yellow Cress**
Rorippa curvisiliqua

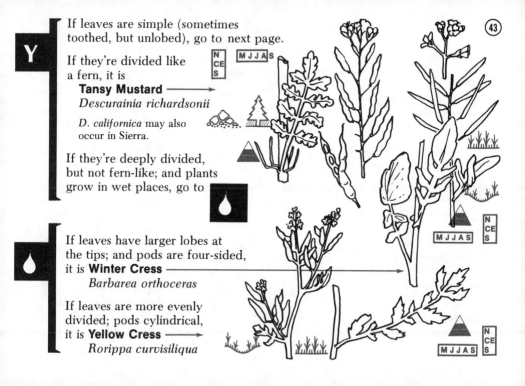

43

If flowers are in spike-like racemes; and pods are long and narrow, it is
Sierra Wallflower ————➤
Erysimum perenne

If flowers are in small clusters or single; plants are low; and pods are broad, rounded, and:

● flat, it is
Whitlow Grass
Draba lemmonii

Other species include:
D. stenoloba, annual; *D. douglasii*, leathery leaves, white flowers; and *D. paysonii*, densely overlapping leaves, pale yellow flowers.

● inflated, it is
Bladderpod ————➤
Lesquerella occidentalis

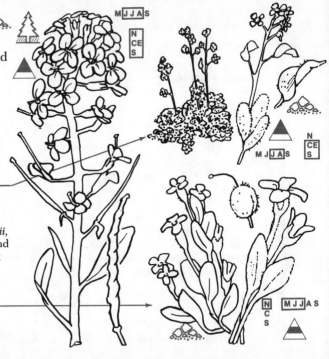

Ericaceae (Heather Family) Usually woody plants. Leaves simple, entire, firm. Flowers have five sepals, five partly fused petals often forming urn shape. Stamens mostly ten, opening by special pores in their ends.

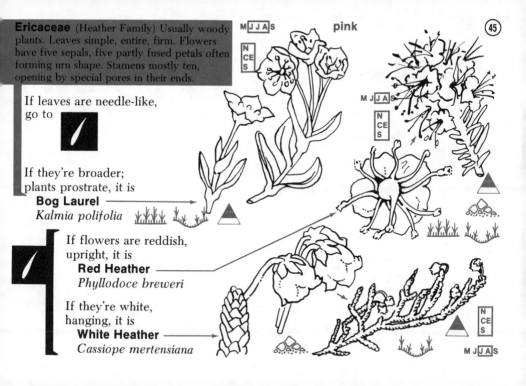

If leaves are needle-like, go to

If they're broader; plants prostrate, it is
Bog Laurel
Kalmia polifolia

If flowers are reddish, upright, it is
Red Heather
Phyllodoce breweri

If they're white, hanging, it is
White Heather
Cassiope mertensiana

(46) **Droseraceae** (Sundew Family) Expanded leaf
blades have upper surface covered by sticky,
gland-tipped hairs. Insects are trapped,
enfolded, digested. Small white
flowers have details like saxifrages.

One Sierra species:
Sundew ⟶
Drosera rotundifolia

Fumariaceae (Fumitory Family) Leaves
highly divided, fern-like. Stems and roots have
orange sap. Irregular flowers have two
tiny sepals, four petals fused at
tips, hiding reproductive parts.

If there are several flowers
on a stalk over 15cm high, it is
Western Bleeding Heart
Dicentra formosa

pink-
purple   pink

If flowers are single, close
to ground, it is **Steer's Head** ⟶
D. uniflora

D. pauciflora is like *D. uniflora*,
but petals recurve only a short way.
D. chrysantha (Golden Eardrops)
may occur in bushy areas.

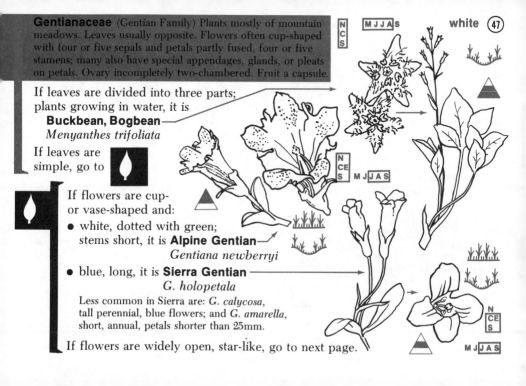

Gentianaceae (Gentian Family) Plants mostly of mountain meadows. Leaves usually opposite. Flowers often cup-shaped with four or five sepals and petals partly fused, four or five stamens; many also have special appendages, glands, or pleats on petals. Ovary incompletely two-chambered. Fruit a capsule.

white (47)

If leaves are divided into three parts; plants growing in water, it is **Buckbean, Bogbean** *Menyanthes trifoliata*

If leaves are simple, go to

If flowers are cup- or vase-shaped and:

● white, dotted with green; stems short, it is **Alpine Gentian** *Gentiana newberryi*

● blue, long, it is **Sierra Gentian** *G. holopetala*

Less common in Sierra are: *G. calycosa*, tall perennial, blue flowers; and *G. amarella*, short, annual, petals shorter than 25mm.

If flowers are widely open, star-like, go to next page.

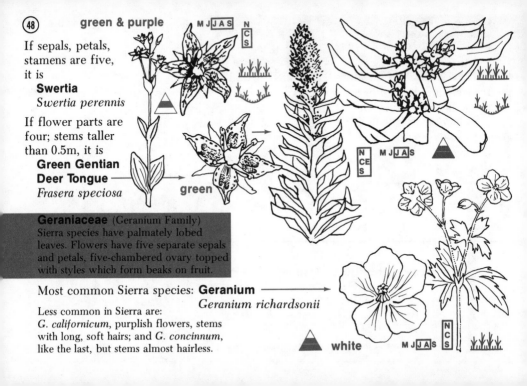

green & purple

If sepals, petals, stamens are five, it is
Swertia
Swertia perennis

If flower parts are four; stems taller than 0.5m, it is
Green Gentian
Deer Tongue
Frasera speciosa

green

Geraniaceae (Geranium Family) Sierra species have palmately lobed leaves. Flowers have five separate sepals and petals, five-chambered ovary topped with styles which form beaks on fruit.

Most common Sierra species: **Geranium**
Geranium richardsonii

Less common in Sierra are:
G. californicum, purplish flowers, stems with long, soft hairs; and *G. concinnum*, like the last, but stems almost hairless.

white

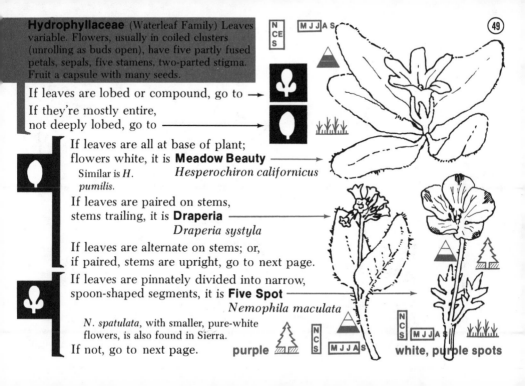

Hydrophyllaceae (Waterleaf Family) Leaves variable. Flowers, usually in coiled clusters (unrolling as buds open), have five partly fused petals, sepals, five stamens, two-parted stigma. Fruit a capsule with many seeds.

If leaves are lobed or compound, go to →

If they're mostly entire, not deeply lobed, go to →

If leaves are all at base of plant; flowers white, it is **Meadow Beauty** →
Hesperochiron californicus

Similar is *H. pumilis.*

If leaves are paired on stems, stems trailing, it is **Draperia** →
Draperia systyla

If leaves are alternate on stems; or, if paired, stems are upright, go to next page.

If leaves are pinnately divided into narrow, spoon-shaped segments, it is **Five Spot** →
Nemophila maculata

N. spatulata, with smaller, pure-white flowers, is also found in Sierra.

If not, go to next page.

purple

white, purple spots

dull purple

bluish

If leaves are clustered
near base of plant, it is ·
Waterleaf
Hydrophyllum occidentale

If leaves are distributed
along stems, go to ———→

 If leaves
are undivided, it is
Phacelia ————→
Phacelia racemosa

If they're twice divided
(divisions have divisions),
go to
 next page

If they're once divided,
go to
 next page

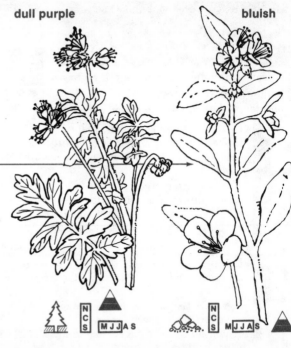

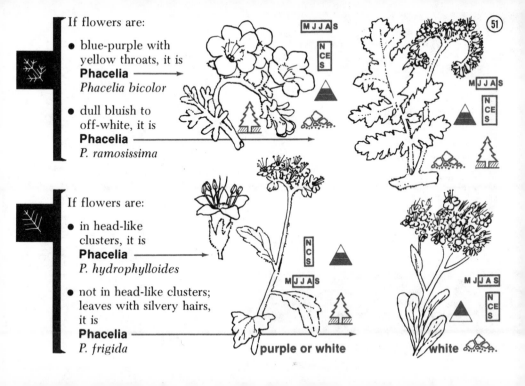

⑤

If flowers are:

- blue-purple with yellow throats, it is **Phacelia** ⟶ *Phacelia bicolor*

- dull bluish to off-white, it is **Phacelia** ⟶ *P. ramosissima*

If flowers are:

- in head-like clusters, it is **Phacelia** ⟶ *P. hydrophylloides*

- not in head-like clusters; leaves with silvery hairs, it is **Phacelia** ⟶ *P. frigida*

purple or white

white

52 **Hypericaceae** (St Johnswort Family)
Entire, opposite leaves, with tiny black glands.
Flowers have five free sepals and petals,
numerous stamens clustered in bunches,
and compound pistil. Fruit a capsule.

If flowers are salmon-yellow,
tiny; plant grows close to
ground, it is
Tinker's Penny
Hypericum anagalloides

If flowers are bright
yellow, conspicuous;
plant upright, it is
St Johnswort ———
H. formosum

M J J A S   N C S

Iridaceae (Iris Family) Sword-like leaves are
arranged in flattened sprays so that bases overlap.
Flowers have three colored sepals and petals
and three stamens, styles and stigmas. Ovary
is inferior, three-chambered. Fruit a capsule.

(Iris family is on next page.)

M J J A S   N C E S

If there are conspicuous, drooping sepals and upright petals; and flowers are:

- pale yellow to purple, growing in pine forest, it is **Sierra Iris Rainbow Iris** *Iris hartwegii* →

- blue-violet, growing in high meadow, it is **Meadow Iris** ——— *Iris missouriensis*

If petals and sepals look alike; flowers are blue-purple with yellow centers, it is **Mountain Blue-eyed Grass** *Sisyrinchium idahoense*

Similar, but with yellow flowers is *S. elmeri* (Yellow-eyed Grass).

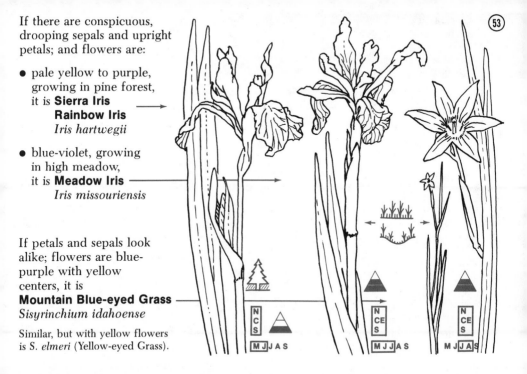

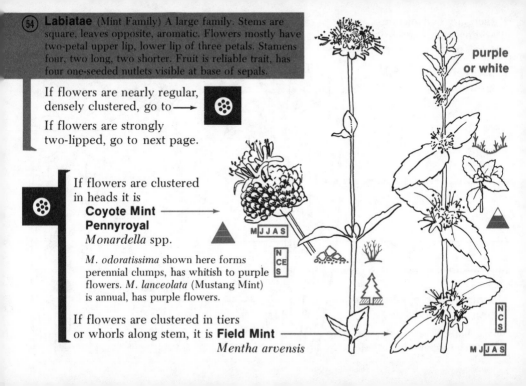

(54) Labiatae (Mint Family) A large family. Stems are square, leaves opposite, aromatic. Flowers mostly have two-petal upper lip, lower lip of three petals. Stamens four, two long, two shorter. Fruit is reliable trait, has four one-seeded nutlets visible at base of sepals.

If flowers are nearly regular, densely clustered, go to →

If flowers are strongly two-lipped, go to next page.

purple or white

If flowers are clustered in heads it is
Coyote Mint
Pennyroyal →
Monardella spp.

M. odoratissima shown here forms perennial clumps, has whitish to purple flowers. *M. lanceolata* (Mustang Mint) is annual, has purple flowers.

If flowers are clustered in tiers or whorls along stem, it is **Field Mint** →
Mentha arvensis

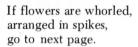

If flowers are whorled,
arranged in spikes,
go to next page.

If flowers are in small
groups, and:

- flowers look like
  Snapdragons, it is
  Skullcap ⟶
  Scutellaria californica

- foliage is strong-
  smelling; stamens
  curled, it is
  Blue Curls ⟶
  Trichostema oblongum

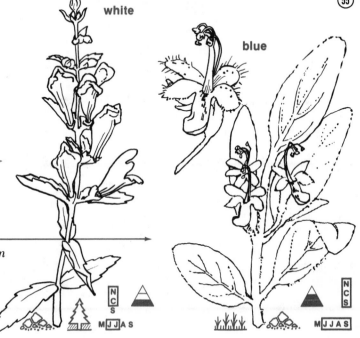

⑤⑤

white

blue

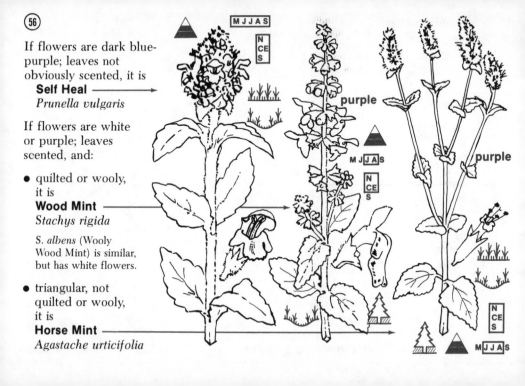

If flowers are dark blue-purple; leaves not obviously scented, it is
Self Heal ——————⟶
Prunella vulgaris

If flowers are white or purple; leaves scented, and:

● quilted or wooly, it is
Wood Mint ——————⟶
Stachys rigida

S. *albens* (Wooly Wood Mint) is similar, but has white flowers.

● triangular, not quilted or wooly, it is
Horse Mint ——————⟶
Agastache urticifolia

purple

purple

M J J A S

N C E S

M J J A S

N C E S

N C E S

M J J A S

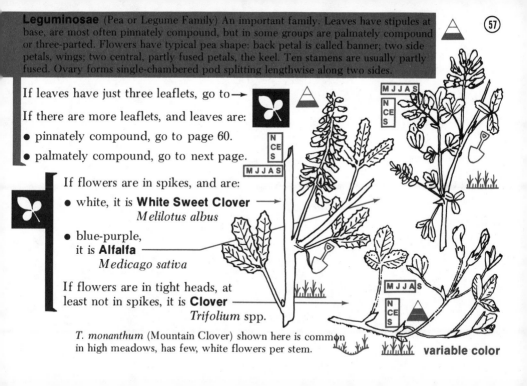

Leguminosae (Pea or Legume Family) An important family. Leaves have stipules at base, are most often pinnately compound, but in some groups are palmately compound or three-parted. Flowers have typical pea shape: back petal is called banner; two side petals, wings; two central, partly fused petals, the keel. Ten stamens are usually partly fused. Ovary forms single-chambered pod splitting lengthwise along two sides.

If leaves have just three leaflets, go to →

If there are more leaflets, and leaves are:

- pinnately compound, go to page 60.
- palmately compound, go to next page.

If flowers are in spikes, and are:

- white, it is **White Sweet Clover** →
  Melilotus albus

- blue-purple,
  it is **Alfalfa** ——
  Medicago sativa

If flowers are in tight heads, at
least not in spikes, it is **Clover** ——
  Trifolium spp.

T. monanthum (Mountain Clover) shown here is common
in high meadows, has few, white flowers per stem.

variable color

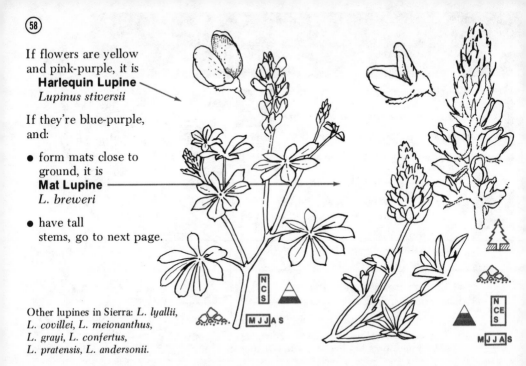

If flowers are yellow
and pink-purple, it is
Harlequin Lupine
Lupinus stiversii

If they're blue-purple,
and:

- form mats close to
  ground, it is
  Mat Lupine
  L. breweri

- have tall
  stems, go to next page.

Other lupines in Sierra: *L. lyallii,*
L. covillei, L. meionanthus,
L. grayi, L. confertus,
L. pratensis, L. andersonii.

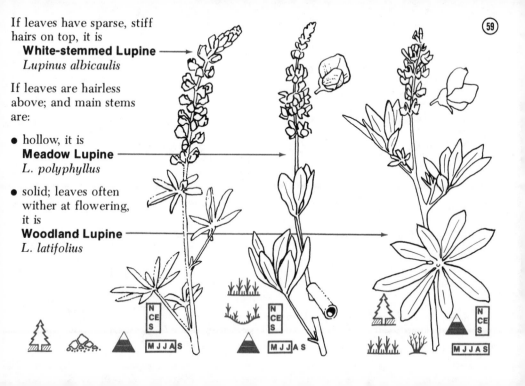

If leaves have sparse, stiff hairs on top, it is
White-stemmed Lupine
Lupinus albicaulis

If leaves are hairless above; and main stems are:

● hollow, it is
Meadow Lupine
L. polyphyllus

● solid; leaves often wither at flowering, it is
Woodland Lupine
L. latifolius

59

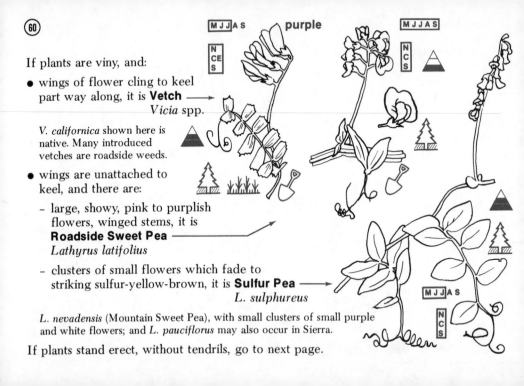

purple

If plants are viny, and:

● wings of flower cling to keel part way along, it is **Vetch** ——→
Vicia spp.

V. californica shown here is native. Many introduced vetches are roadside weeds.

● wings are unattached to keel, and there are:

– large, showy, pink to purplish flowers, winged stems, it is **Roadside Sweet Pea** ——→
Lathyrus latifolius

– clusters of small flowers which fade to striking sulfur-yellow-brown, it is **Sulfur Pea** ——→
L. sulphureus

L. nevadensis (Mountain Sweet Pea), with small clusters of small purple and white flowers; and *L. pauciflorus* may also occur in Sierra.

If plants stand erect, without tendrils, go to next page.

If flowers are in racemes, see *Astragalus*, next page.

If flowers are in racemes, see *Astragalus*, next page.

If flowers are in umbels or single,
and are:

- greenish tinged with
  purple; leaflets
  coarse, it is
  Lotus ——————→
  Lotus crassifolius

- yellow and white,
  it is
  Meadow Lotus ——→
  L. oblongifolius

- bright yellow;
  makes hairy mats
  it is
  Wooly Lotus ————
  L. nevadensis

Also in Sierra: *L pinnatus,
L. humistratus.*

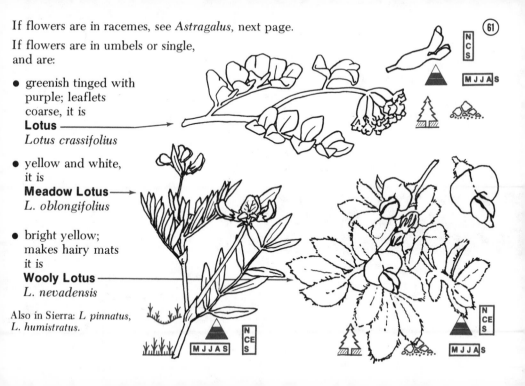

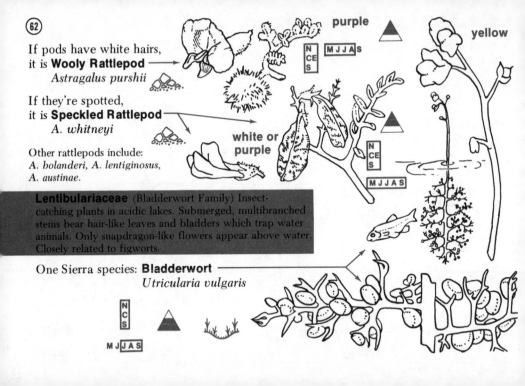

(62)

If pods have white hairs,
it is **Wooly Rattlepod** →
  Astragalus purshii

If they're spotted,
it is **Speckled Rattlepod** →
  A. whitneyi

Other rattlepods include:
*A. bolanderi, A. lentiginosus,
A. austinae.*

purple

yellow

**white or
purple**

Lentibulariaceae (Bladderwort Family) Insect-
catching plants in acidic lakes. Submerged, multibranched
stems bear hair-like leaves and bladders which trap water
animals. Only snapdragon-like flowers appear above water.
Closely related to figworts.

One Sierra species: **Bladderwort** →
  Utricularia vulgaris

Liliaceae (Lily Family) Plants mostly grow from fleshy, underground tubers, corms, bulbs. Flowers in racemes or panicles. Most have three sepals and petals which look alike. Stamens are six, stigma three-lobed, ovary three-chambered. Fruit a capsule or berry.

If there are three broad, net-veined leaves, it is
Wake Robin
Trillium chloropetalum

If leaves are:

- pleated; and plants are at least 1m tall, it is
Corn Lily
False Hellebore
Veratrum californicum

- narrow, often grass-like, go to next page

- broader, not grass-like, go to next page

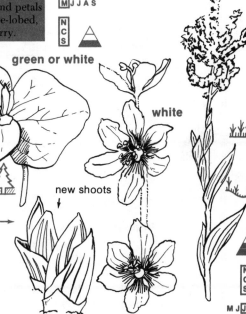

green or white

white

new shoots

If leaves are:

- wavy-edged; flowers opening
  late afternoon, it is
  Amole, Soap Plant ————
  Chlorogalum pomeridianum

white

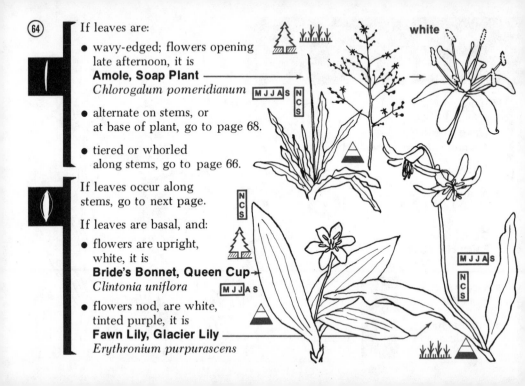

- alternate on stems, or
  at base of plant, go to page 68.

- tiered or whorled
  along stems, go to page 66.

If leaves occur along
stems, go to next page.

If leaves are basal, and:

- flowers are upright,
  white, it is
  Bride's Bonnet, Queen Cup →
  Clintonia uniflora

- flowers nod, are white,
  tinted purple, it is
  Fawn Lily, Glacier Lily ————
  Erythronium purpurascens

If flowers hang under leaves, it is **Fairy Bells** ————
Disporum hookeri

If they're clustered beyond
leaves, and grow in:

- racemes, it is
  Slim False Solomon's Seal —
  S. stellata

- dense panicles, it is
  Fat False Solomon's Seal —
  Smilacina racemosa

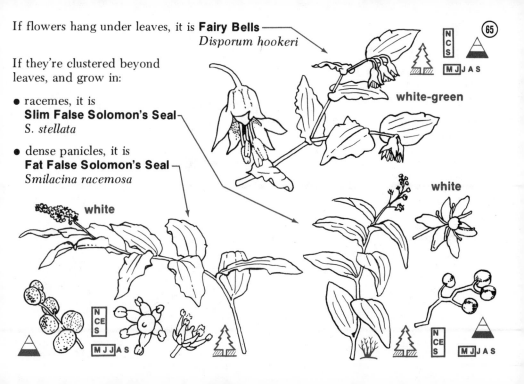

white-green

white

white

65

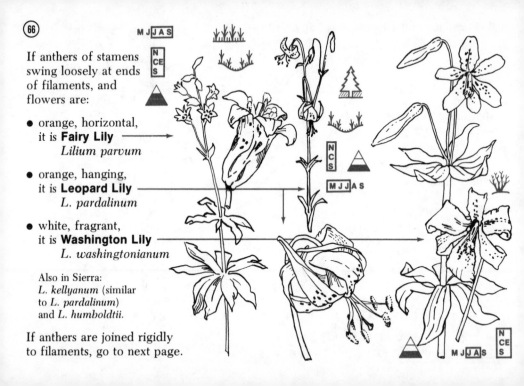

If anthers of stamens swing loosely at ends of filaments, and flowers are:

- orange, horizontal, it is **Fairy Lily** ⟶
  Lilium parvum

- orange, hanging, it is **Leopard Lily** ⟶
  L. pardalinum

- white, fragrant, it is **Washington Lily** ⟶
  L. washingtonianum

Also in Sierra:
L. kellyanum (similar to *L. pardalinum*) and *L. humboldtii*.

If anthers are joined rigidly to filaments, go to next page.

If flowers are orange-red, it is **Scarlet Fritillary** ⟶ *Fritillaria recurva*

If they're brownish-purple, checkered, it is **Alpine Checker Lily** ⟶ *F. atropurpurea*

Other Sierra species include: *F. pinetorum* (Pine Fritillary), like *F. atropurpurea;* and *F. micrantha*, with small brownish or greenish, hanging flowers.

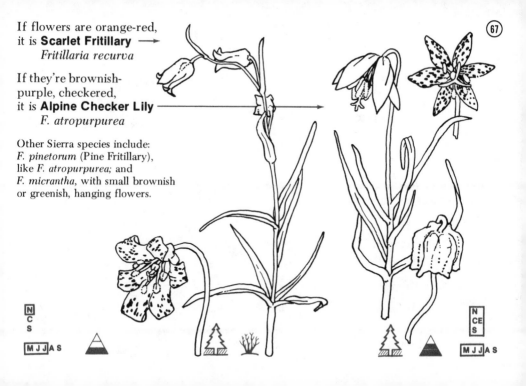

N
C
S

M J J A S

N
C E
S

M J J A S

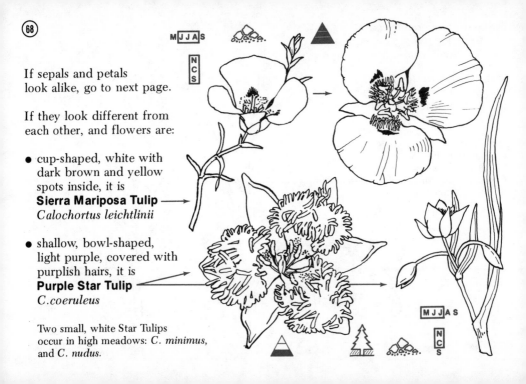

If sepals and petals look alike, go to next page.

If they look different from each other, and flowers are:

- cup-shaped, white with dark brown and yellow spots inside, it is **Sierra Mariposa Tulip** —→ *Calochortus leichtlinii*

- shallow, bowl-shaped, light purple, covered with purplish hairs, it is **Purple Star Tulip** —→ *C.coeruleus*

Two small, white Star Tulips occur in high meadows: *C. minimus*, and *C. nudus*.

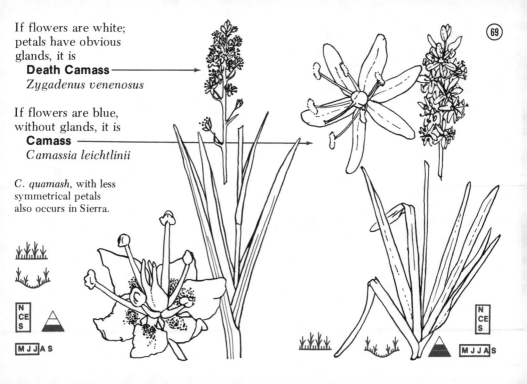

If flowers are white; petals have obvious glands, it is
Death Camass ──────▶
Zygadenus venenosus

If flowers are blue, without glands, it is
Camass ──────▶
Camassia leichtlinii

C. quamash, with less symmetrical petals also occurs in Sierra.

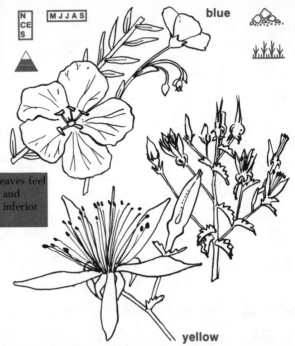

⑦ Linaceae (Flax Family) Flowers have five separate sepals and petals, five stamens. Petals fall at the slightest touch. Five styles on five-chambered ovary. Fruit a capsule.

Most common Sierra species:
Blue Flax
Linum lewisii

L. digynum also occurs.

Loasaceae (Blazing Star Family) Leaves feel sandpapery. Flowers have five sepals and petals, numerous stamens in bunches, inferior ovary. Fruit a many-seeded capsule.

One Sierra species:
Blazing Star
Mentzelia laevicaulis

blue

yellow

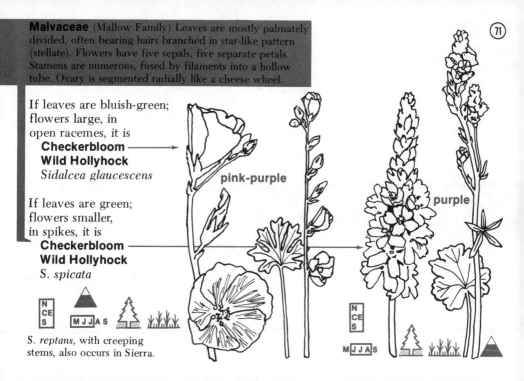

Malvaceae (Mallow Family) Leaves are mostly palmately divided, often bearing hairs branched in star-like pattern (stellate). Flowers have five sepals, five separate petals. Stamens are numerous, fused by filaments into a hollow tube. Ovary is segmented radially like a cheese wheel.

If leaves are bluish-green; flowers large, in open racemes, it is
Checkerbloom
Wild Hollyhock
Sidalcea glaucescens

pink-purple

purple

If leaves are green; flowers smaller, in spikes, it is
Checkerbloom
Wild Hollyhock
S. spicata

S. reptans, with creeping stems, also occurs in Sierra.

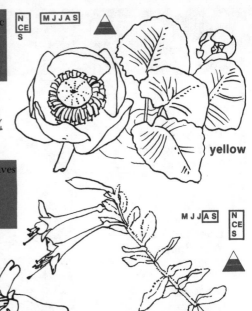

(72) **Nymphaeaceae** (Water Lily Family) Aquatic plants. Roots and stems anchored in mud; leaf blades float. Flowers have sepals grading into petals, numerous stamens, conspicuous central pistil of many fused parts.

One common Sierra species:
Yellow Pond Lily
Nuphar polysepalum

Less common is *Brasenia schreberi* (Water Shield) with purple flowers.

yellow

Onagraceae (Evening Primrose Family) Leaves simple, often entire. Four separate sepals and petals sometimes forming tube. Eight stamens, solid or four-lobed stigma, inferior, four-chambered ovary. Fruit a capsule.

If flowers are bright red, trumpet-shaped, it is **California Fuchsia**
Zauschneria californica

If not, go to next page.

If flowers are:

- purple to pink,
  go to next page.

- whitish, stems thread-like,
  it is **Gayophytum** ⟶
  Gayophytum nuttallii

  A few similar species
  also occur in Sierra.

- yellow, with:

  – basal leaves, flowers
    close to ground, it is
    Evening Primrose ⟶
    Oenothera heterantha

  – tall, leafy stems, flowers
    above leaves, it is
    Evening Primrose ⟶
    O. hookeri

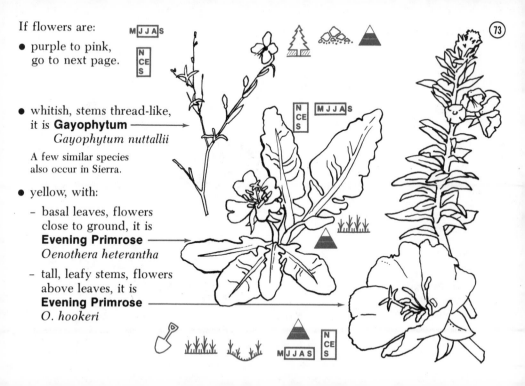

If sepals turn to one
side of flower, go to
next page.

If sepals are symmetrical;
and the plant:

- has tall racemes of flowers,
  it is **Willow Herb, Fireweed** ——————▶
  Epilobium angustifolium

  Many smaller-flowered, similar-looking
  willow herbs occur in Sierra: *E. paniculatum,*
  E. glandulosum, E. exaltatum, E. brevistylum,
  E. pringleanum, E. glaberrimum,
  E. anagallidifolium, E. hornemannii,
  E. lactiflorum, E. adenocaulon.

- forms sprawling mounds,
  it is **Rockfringe**
  Purple Mats ——————————▶
  E. obcordatum

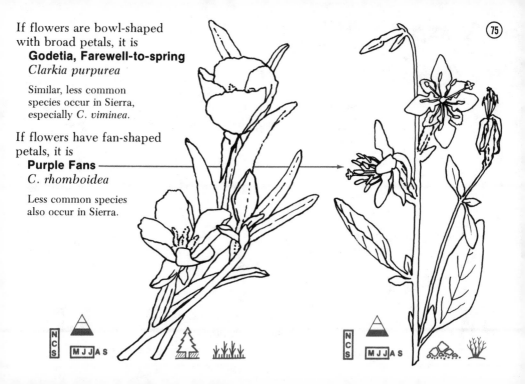

If flowers are bowl-shaped
with broad petals, it is
Godetia, Farewell-to-spring
Clarkia purpurea

Similar, less common
species occur in Sierra,
especially *C. viminea*.

If flowers have fan-shaped
petals, it is
Purple Fans
C. rhomboidea

Less common species
also occur in Sierra.

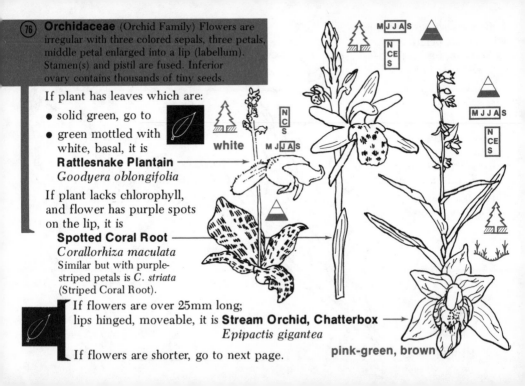

(76) **Orchidaceae** (Orchid Family) Flowers are irregular with three colored sepals, three petals, middle petal enlarged into a lip (labellum). Stamen(s) and pistil are fused. Inferior ovary contains thousands of tiny seeds.

If plant has leaves which are:

- solid green, go to

- green mottled with white, basal, it is **Rattlesnake Plantain** *Goodyera oblongifolia*

white

If plant lacks chlorophyll, and flower has purple spots on the lip, it is

Spotted Coral Root *Corallorhiza maculata* Similar but with purple-striped petals is *C. striata* (Striped Coral Root).

If flowers are over 25mm long; lips hinged, moveable, it is **Stream Orchid, Chatterbox** *Epipactis gigantea*

If flowers are shorter, go to next page.

pink-green, brown

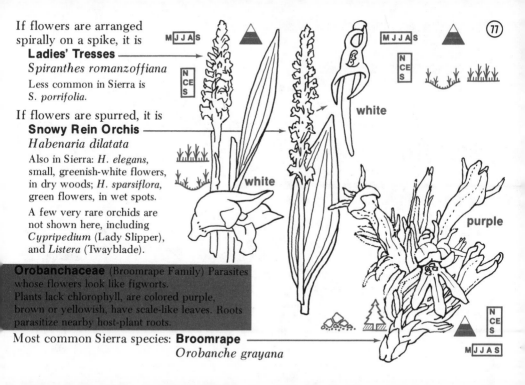

If flowers are arranged spirally on a spike, it is
Ladies' Tresses
Spiranthes romanzoffiana
Less common in Sierra is
S. *porrifolia.*

If flowers are spurred, it is
Snowy Rein Orchis
Habenaria dilatata
Also in Sierra: *H. elegans*, small, greenish-white flowers, in dry woods; *H. sparsiflora*, green flowers, in wet spots.

A few very rare orchids are not shown here, including *Cypripedium* (Lady Slipper), and *Listera* (Twayblade).

Orobanchaceae (Broomrape Family) Parasites whose flowers look like figworts. Plants lack chlorophyll, are colored purple, brown or yellowish, have scale-like leaves. Roots parasitize nearby host-plant roots.

Most common Sierra species: **Broomrape**
Orobanche grayana

white

white

purple

M J J A s
N C E S

M J J A s
N C E S

N C E S
M J J A S

(77)

(78) **Paeoniaceae** (Peony Family)
Closely related to buttercups. Principal
difference is direction of development
of the numerous stamens, and sepals
which remain on flower even in fruit.

One Sierra species: **Wild Peony** ——
Paeonia brownii
maroon-red

Papaveraceae (Poppy Family) Sepals,
which fall as bud opens, are usually half
the number of petals. Petals are free,
often crinkled, four to six. Stamens are
numerous, pistil compound, fruit a capsule.

If leaves are:

- much divided, ferny;
  flowers orange-yellow,
  it is
  California Poppy ——
  Eschscholzia californica

- very spiny; flowers
  snowy white, it is
  Prickly Poppy ——
  Argemone munita

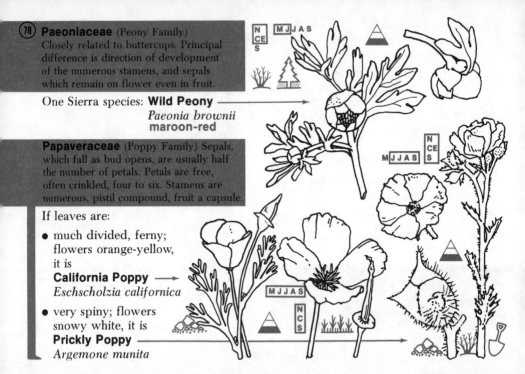

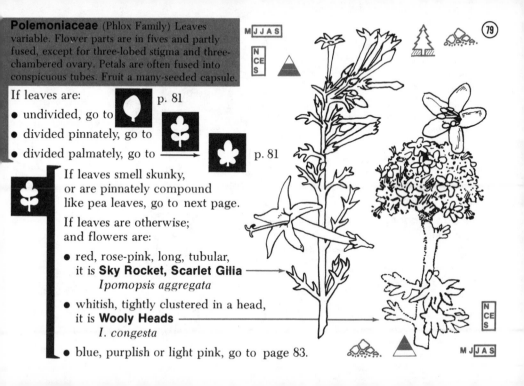

Polemoniaceae (Phlox Family) Leaves variable. Flower parts are in fives and partly fused, except for three-lobed stigma and three-chambered ovary. Petals are often fused into conspicuous tubes. Fruit a many-seeded capsule.

If leaves are:

- undivided, go to   p. 81
- divided pinnately, go to
- divided palmately, go to   p. 81

If leaves smell skunky, or are pinnately compound like pea leaves, go to next page.

If leaves are otherwise; and flowers are:

- red, rose-pink, long, tubular, it is **Sky Rocket, Scarlet Gilia** ⟶ *Ipomopsis aggregata*
- whitish, tightly clustered in a head, it is **Wooly Heads** ⟶ *I. congesta*
- blue, purplish or light pink, go to page 83.

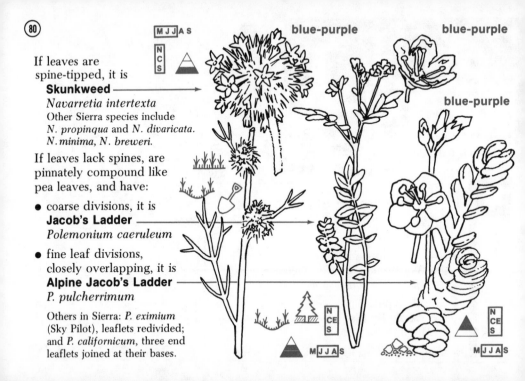

blue-purple **blue-purple**

blue-purple

If leaves are
spine-tipped, it is
Skunkweed ⟶
Navarretia intertexta
Other Sierra species include
N. propinqua and *N. divaricata.*
N. minima, N. breweri.

If leaves lack spines, are
pinnately compound like
pea leaves, and have:

- coarse divisions, it is
Jacob's Ladder ⟶
Polemonium caeruleum

- fine leaf divisions,
closely overlapping, it is
Alpine Jacob's Ladder ⟶
P. pulcherrimum

Others in Sierra: *P. eximium*
(Sky Pilot), leaflets redivided;
and *P. californicum*, three end
leaflets joined at their bases.

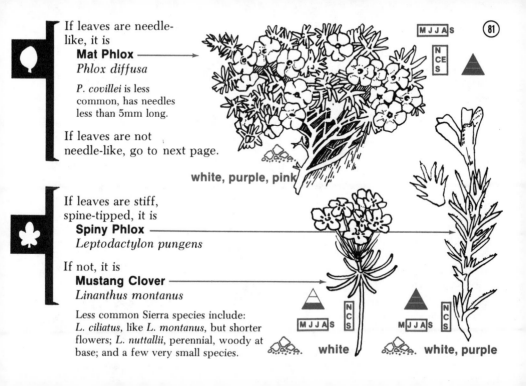

If leaves are needle-like, it is
Mat Phlox ———
Phlox diffusa

P. covillei is less common, has needles less than 5mm long.

If leaves are not needle-like, go to next page.

white, purple, pink

MJJAS

N C E S

If leaves are stiff, spine-tipped, it is
Spiny Phlox ———
Leptodactylon pungens

If not, it is
Mustang Clover ———
Linanthus montanus

Less common Sierra species include:
L. ciliatus, like *L. montanus*, but shorter flowers; *L. nuttallii*, perennial, woody at base; and a few very small species.

MJJAS   N C S   **white**

MJJAS   N C S   **white, purple**

If plants are woody at base;
flowers pinkish, it is
Showy Phlox ———→
Phlox speciosa

If plants aren't woody
and flowers are:

• clustered in tight
heads, it is
Bride's Bouquet ————
Collomia grandiflora

C. tinctoria and *C. linearis*
are less common, have
purplish flowers.

• scattered, go to next page.

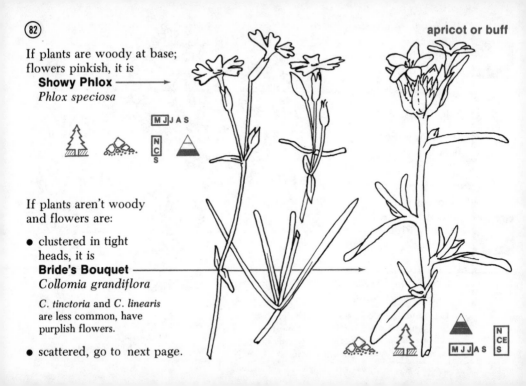

If flowers are bluish,
in tight heads, it is
Pincushion Gilia
Gilia capitata

If they're pinkish to
purplish, scattered,
about 13mm long, it is
Gilia
G. leptalea

Also in Sierra:
G. capillaris, thread-like
stems and flowers less
than 7mm long;
G. leptantha, pinkish
flowers up to 25mm long,
cobwebby hairs at base
of plant.

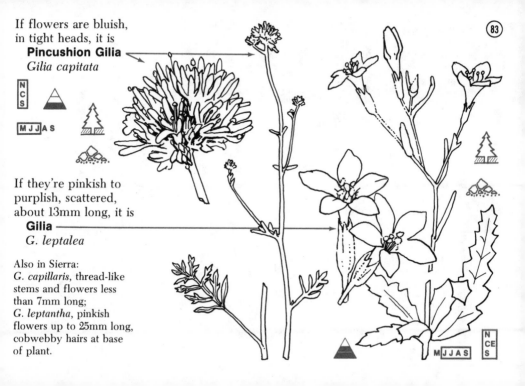

Polygonaceae (Buckwheat Family) Leaves (except
Eriogonum), bear papery stipules (ochrae). Small, often three-
parted flowers are composed of colored sepals, with stamens
to match number of sepals. Arrangement of flowers may
be important in identification. Most consistent family
feature is small, one-seeded fruit (achene) with three sides.

**green or
reddish**

If leaves have obvious
papery stipules, go to

If not, go to page 86.

 reddish

If leaves are kidney-
shaped, basal, it is
Mountain Sorrel
Oxyria digyna ⟶

If leaves are some other
shape, and flowers
have:

- four or six
  sepals, it is
  Dock ⟶
  Rumex californicus

- five sepals, go to next page.

If flowers are:

- pink, growing in
  water, it is
  Water Knotweed
  Smartweed
  Polygonum coccineum

- white, in dense
  spikes, it is
  Bistort
  P. bistortoides

- greenish, red stems,
  broad leaves, it is
  Green-flowered Knotweed
  P. davisiae

Other Sierra species:
P. douglasii, P. kelloggii,
P. shastense,
P. phytolaccaefolium.

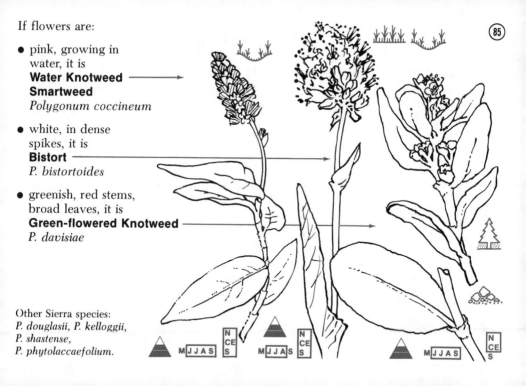

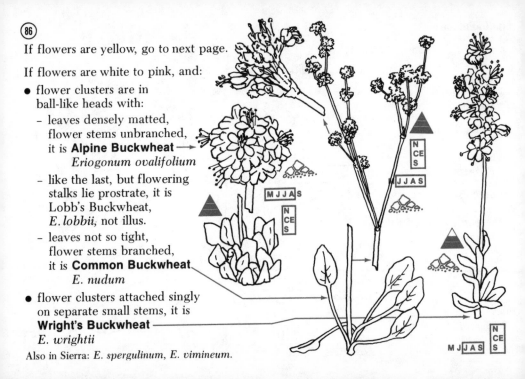

If flowers are yellow, go to next page.

If flowers are white to pink, and:

- flower clusters are in ball-like heads with:
  - leaves densely matted, flower stems unbranched, it is **Alpine Buckwheat** →
    Eriogonum ovalifolium
  - like the last, but flowering stalks lie prostrate, it is Lobb's Buckwheat, *E. lobbii,* not illus.
  - leaves not so tight, flower stems branched, it is **Common Buckwheat** *E. nudum*
- flower clusters attached singly on separate small stems, it is **Wright's Buckwheat** *E. wrightii*

Also in Sierra: *E. spergulinum, E. vimineum.*

If sepals stand up,
it is
   Sulfur Flower ———————→
   Eriogonum marifolium

If they turn down,
it is
   Sulfur Flower ———————————————→
   E. umbellatum

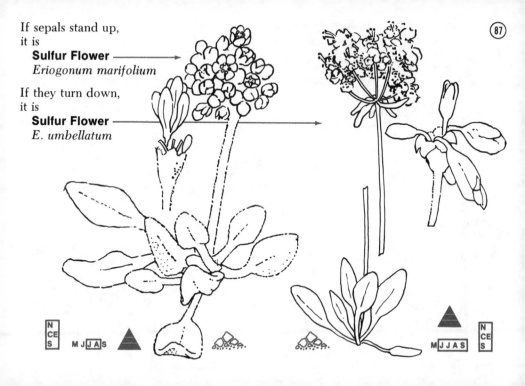

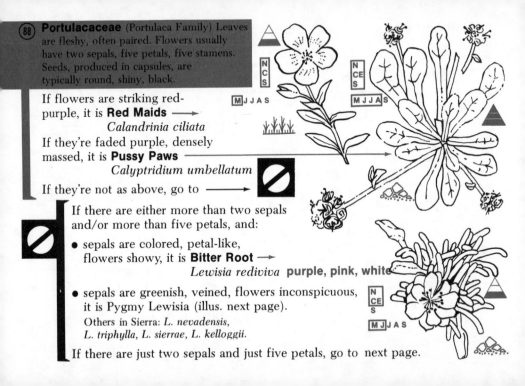

(88) **Portulacaceae** (Portulaca Family) Leaves are fleshy, often paired. Flowers usually have two sepals, five petals, five stamens. Seeds, produced in capsules, are typically round, shiny, black.

If flowers are striking red-purple, it is **Red Maids** ⟶
    Calandrinia ciliata

If they're faded purple, densely massed, it is **Pussy Paws** ⟶
    Calyptridium umbellatum

If they're not as above, go to ⟶

If there are either more than two sepals and/or more than five petals, and:

- sepals are colored, petal-like, flowers showy, it is **Bitter Root** ⟶
  Lewisia rediviva **purple, pink, white**

- sepals are greenish, veined, flowers inconspicuous, it is Pygmy Lewisia (illus. next page).
  Others in Sierra: *L. nevadensis, L. triphylla, L. sierrae, L. kelloggii.*

If there are just two sepals and just five petals, go to next page.

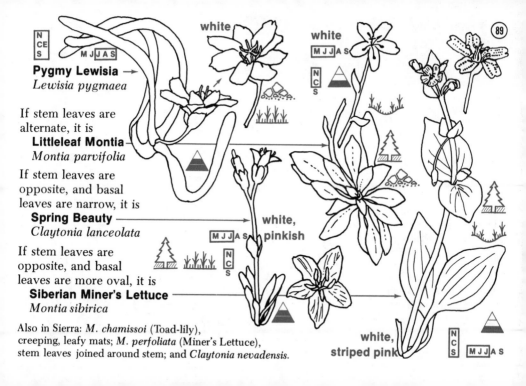

Pygmy Lewisia →
Lewisia pygmaea

white

white

If stem leaves are
alternate, it is
Littleleaf Montia
Montia parvifolia

If stem leaves are
opposite, and basal
leaves are narrow, it is
Spring Beauty
Claytonia lanceolata

white,
pinkish

If stem leaves are
opposite, and basal
leaves are more oval, it is
Siberian Miner's Lettuce
Montia sibirica

Also in Sierra: *M. chamissoi* (Toad-lily),
creeping, leafy mats; *M. perfoliata* (Miner's Lettuce),
stem leaves joined around stem; and *Claytonia nevadensis*.

white,
striped pink

(90) **Primulaceae** (Primrose Family) Leaves are basal, paired or whorled. Flowers have four to six sepals and petals, fused (sometimes minutely) at bases. Stamens equal petals in number. Fruit a capsule bearing seeds on central column or stalk.

If leaves are:

- whorled at end of short stem; flowers star-like, it is **Star Flower** → *Trientalis latifolia*

- along stems; stems creep, it is **Sierra Primrose** → *Primula suffrutescens*

- basal; petals turn back, it is **Shooting Star** → *Dodecatheon subalpinum*

Also in Sierra: *D. alpinum, D. jeffreyi*. (large upright leaves).

white, pink

pink-purple

red-purple

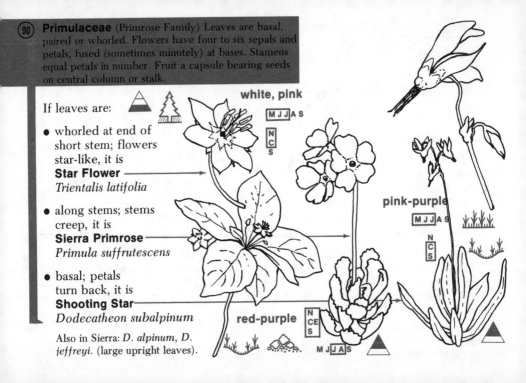

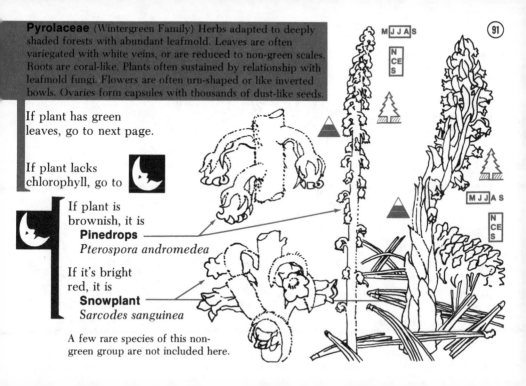

Pyrolaceae (Wintergreen Family) Herbs adapted to deeply shaded forests with abundant leafmold. Leaves are often variegated with white veins, or are reduced to non-green scales. Roots are coral-like. Plants often sustained by relationship with leafmold fungi. Flowers are often urn-shaped or like inverted bowls. Ovaries form capsules with thousands of dust-like seeds.

If plant has green leaves, go to next page.

If plant lacks chlorophyll, go to

If plant is brownish, it is **Pinedrops** *Pterospora andromedea*

If it's bright red, it is **Snowplant** *Sarcodes sanguinea*

A few rare species of this non-green group are not included here.

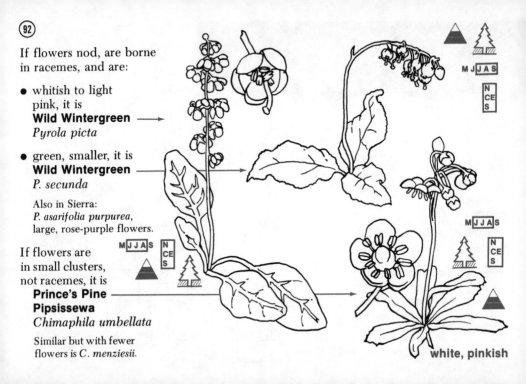

If flowers nod, are borne
in racemes, and are:

- whitish to light
  pink, it is
  Wild Wintergreen →
  Pyrola picta

- green, smaller, it is
  Wild Wintergreen
  P. secunda

  Also in Sierra:
  P. asarifolia purpurea,
  large, rose-purple flowers.

If flowers are
in small clusters,
not racemes, it is
Prince's Pine
Pipsissewa
Chimaphila umbellata

Similar but with fewer
flowers is *C. menziesii*.

white, pinkish

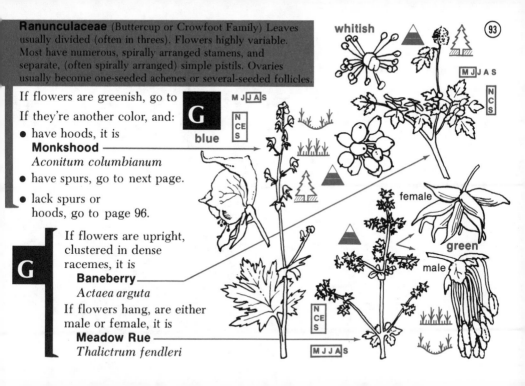

Ranunculaceae (Buttercup or Crowfoot Family) Leaves usually divided (often in threes). Flowers highly variable. Most have numerous, spirally arranged stamens, and separate, (often spirally arranged) simple pistils. Ovaries usually become one-seeded achenes or several-seeded follicles.

whitish

If flowers are greenish, go to **G**

If they're another color, and:

● have hoods, it is
Monkshood
Aconitum columbianum

● have spurs, go to next page.

● lack spurs or
hoods, go to page 96.

blue

G

If flowers are upright, clustered in dense racemes, it is
Baneberry
Actaea arguta

If flowers hang, are either male or female, it is
Meadow Rue
Thalictrum fendleri

female

green

male

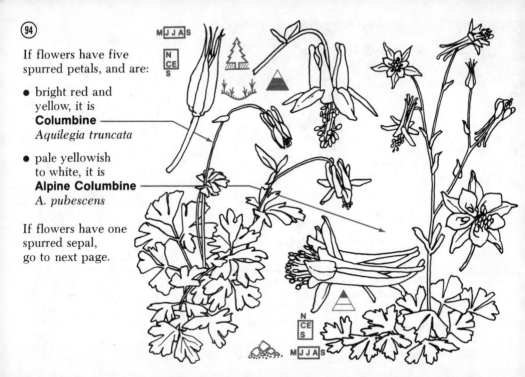

If flowers have five spurred petals, and are:

- bright red and yellow, it is **Columbine** *Aquilegia truncata*

- pale yellowish to white, it is **Alpine Columbine** *A. pubescens*

If flowers have one spurred sepal, go to next page.

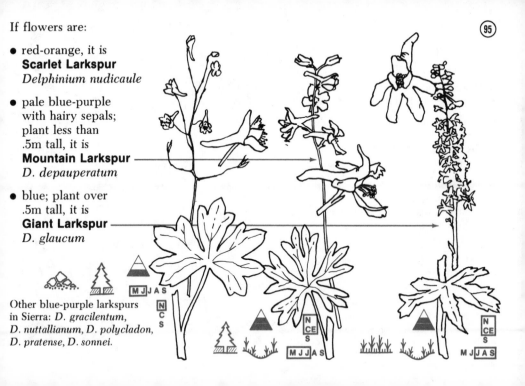

If flowers are:

- red-orange, it is
  Scarlet Larkspur
  Delphinium nudicaule

- pale blue-purple
  with hairy sepals;
  plant less than
  .5m tall, it is
  Mountain Larkspur ⟶
  D. depauperatum

- blue; plant over
  .5m tall, it is
  Giant Larkspur ⟶
  D. glaucum

Other blue-purple larkspurs
in Sierra: *D. gracilentum,*
D. nuttallianum, D. polycladon,
D. pratense, D. sonnei.

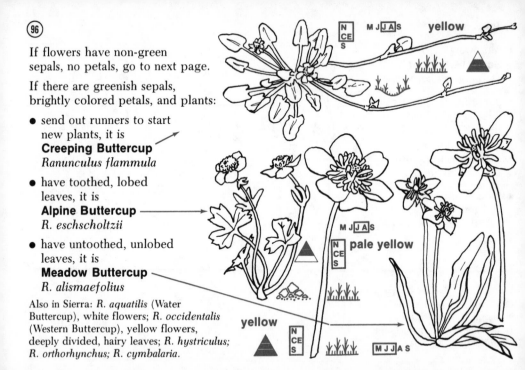

(96)

If flowers have non-green sepals, no petals, go to next page.

If there are greenish sepals, brightly colored petals, and plants:

- send out runners to start new plants, it is
  Creeping Buttercup
  Ranunculus flammula

- have toothed, lobed leaves, it is
  Alpine Buttercup
  R. eschscholtzii

- have untoothed, unlobed leaves, it is
  Meadow Buttercup
  R. alismaefolius

Also in Sierra: *R. aquatilis* (Water Buttercup), white flowers; *R. occidentalis* (Western Buttercup), yellow flowers, deeply divided, hairy leaves; *R. hystriculus; R. orthorhynchus; R. cymbalaria.*

yellow

pale yellow

yellow

If flowers are cream-colored
(blue in bud); leaves
kidney-shaped, it is
   Marsh Marigold ⟶
   Caltha howellii

If flowers are white,
over 5cm across; leaves
divided, it is
   Western Windflower ⟶
   Anemone occidentalis

A. drummondii, smaller flowers,
inconspicuous styles in fruit,
also occurs in Sierra.

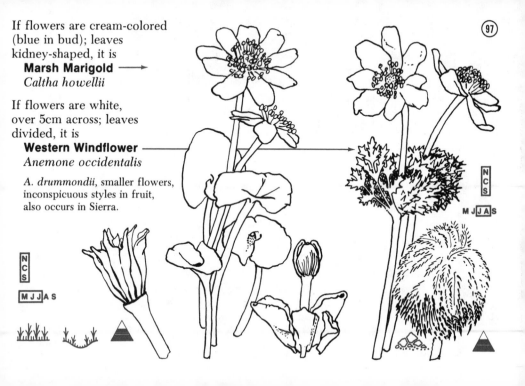

(98) **Rosaceae** (Rose Family) A prominent family. Leaves usually compound and bearing stipules. Flowers have five sepals fused at base into cup, five separate petals, usually numerous stamens. Sepals may appear double, due to row of bracts just below which alternate with them. Pistils vary. In herbaceous kinds they're usually several, separate, with superior ovaries.

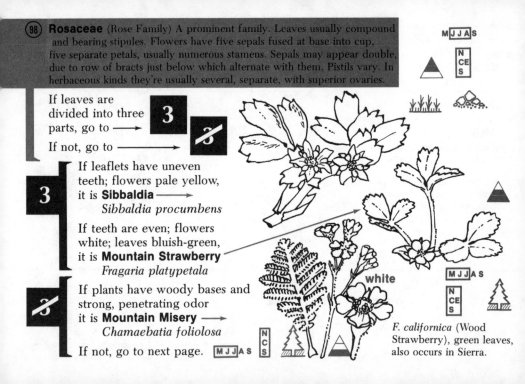

If leaves are divided into three parts, go to → **3**

If not, go to → **3̸**

3

If leaflets have uneven teeth; flowers pale yellow, it is **Sibbaldia** →
Sibbaldia procumbens

If teeth are even; flowers white; leaves bluish-green, it is **Mountain Strawberry**
Fragaria platypetala

3̸

If plants have woody bases and strong, penetrating odor it is **Mountain Misery** →
Chamaebatia foliolosa

If not, go to next page.

white

F. californica (Wood Strawberry), green leaves, also occurs in Sierra.

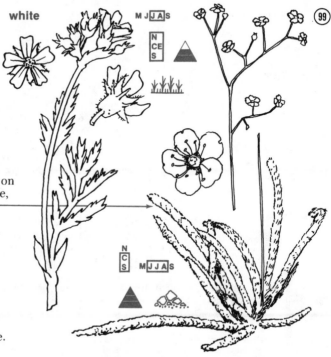

If petals are abruptly
narrowed at their
bases, and leaves are:

● aromatic when crushed,
  it is **Horkelia**
  Horkelia fusca

  H. tridentata is less
  common in Sierra.

● non-aromatic, so finely
  divided they resemble fur on
  a gopher tail; flowers white,
  it is **Rock Potentilla**
  Ivesia santolinoides

Other species in Sierra may
have coarser leaves, and/or
yellow flowers. They include:
*I. pygmaea, I. lycopodioides,
I. gordonii, I. shockleyi,
I. muirii, I. unguiculata.*

If leaves and flowers are
not as above, go to next page.

If flowers droop, have
fuzzy, pink sepals, it is
Pink Plumes ——→
Geum canescens

If flowers are upright, and:

● end leaflet of each
leaf is much larger
than others, it is
Yellow Avens ——
Geum macrophyllum

yellow

● leaflets are about equal
go to

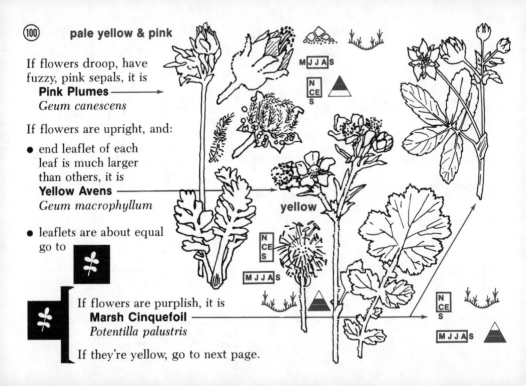

If flowers are purplish, it is
Marsh Cinquefoil ——————→
Potentilla palustris

If they're yellow, go to next page.

If flowers are pale yellow or white; leaves with gland-tipped hairs, it is
Sticky Cinquefoil ———→
Potentilla glandulosa

If flowers are bright yellow; and leaves are:

- palmately divided, it is
Meadow Cinquefoil ———
P. gracilis

- pinnately divided, green above, silvery beneath, it is
Silverweed
P. anserina

- pinnately divided with wooly, white hairs, it is
Brewer's Potentilla ———→
P. breweri

Also in Sierra: *P. drummondii, P. flabellifolia, P. diversifolia, P. pseudosericea.*

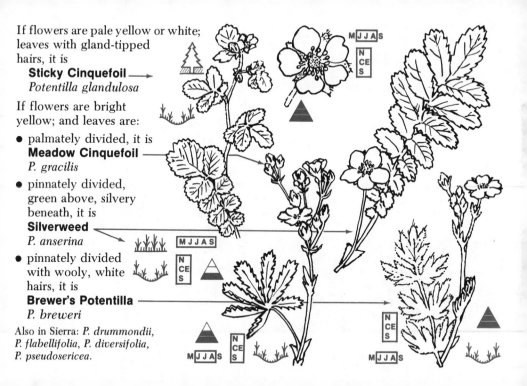

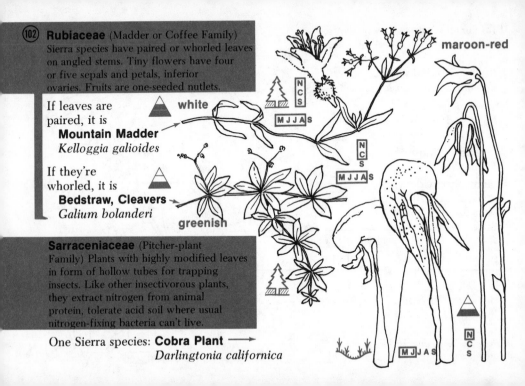

(102) Rubiaceae (Madder or Coffee Family)
Sierra species have paired or whorled leaves
on angled stems. Tiny flowers have four
or five sepals and petals, inferior
ovaries. Fruits are one-seeded nutlets.

If leaves are
paired, it is
Mountain Madder
Kelloggia galioides

white

If they're
whorled, it is
Bedstraw, Cleavers
Galium bolanderi

greenish

maroon-red

Sarraceniaceae (Pitcher-plant
Family) Plants with highly modified leaves
in form of hollow tubes for trapping
insects. Like other insectivorous plants,
they extract nitrogen from animal
protein, tolerate acid soil where usual
nitrogen-fixing bacteria can't live.

One Sierra species: **Cobra Plant**
Darlingtonia californica

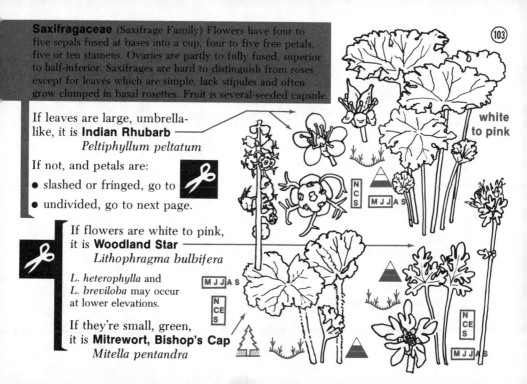

Saxifragaceae (Saxifrage Family) Flowers have four to five sepals fused at bases into a cup, four to five free petals, five or ten stamens. Ovaries are partly to fully fused, superior to half-inferior. Saxifrages are hard to distinguish from roses except for leaves which are simple, lack stipules and often grow clumped in basal rosettes. Fruit is several-seeded capsule.

(103)

white to pink

If leaves are large, umbrella-like, it is **Indian Rhubarb**
Peltiphyllum peltatum

If not, and petals are:

● slashed or fringed, go to ✂

● undivided, go to next page.

If flowers are white to pink, it is **Woodland Star**
Lithophragma bulbifera

L. heterophylla and
L. breviloba may occur
at lower elevations.

If they're small, green, it is **Mitrewort, Bishop's Cap**
Mitella pentandra

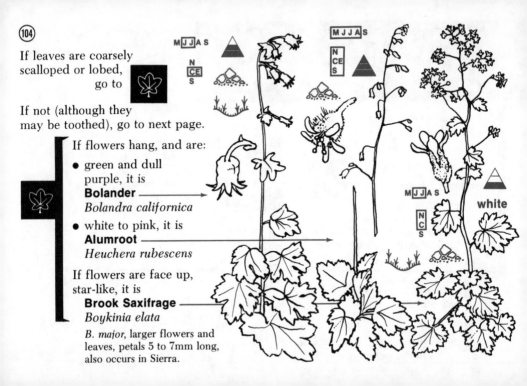

If leaves are coarsely scalloped or lobed, go to

If not (although they may be toothed), go to next page.

If flowers hang, and are:

- green and dull purple, it is **Bolander** *Bolandra californica*

- white to pink, it is **Alumroot** *Heuchera rubescens*

If flowers are face up, star-like, it is **Brook Saxifrage** *Boykinia elata*

B. major, larger flowers and leaves, petals 5 to 7mm long, also occurs in Sierra.

white

If flowers have five pollen-bearing stamens and several gland-tipped, sterile stamens, it is **Grass of Parnassus** *Parnassia palustris*

P. fimbriata, fringed petals, also occurs.

If flowers have ten pollen-bearing stamens (no sterile ones), and:

- leaves are rounded, with coarse teeth, it is **Spotted Saxifrage** *Saxifraga punctata*

- leaves are elliptical, without teeth, it is **Meadow Saxifrage** *S. oregana*

- bulblets replace some flowers; parts tiny, it is **Moss Saxifrage** *S. bryophora*

Also in Sierra: *S. tolmiei*, *S. fallax*, *S. mertensiana*.

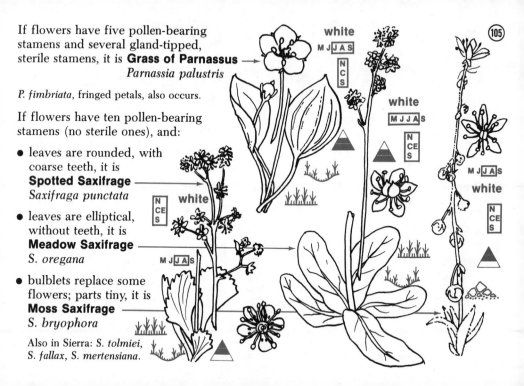

Scrophulariaceae (Figwort or Snapdragon Family) A large, important family. Flowers mostly irregular with upper lip of two petals, lower lip of three. All petals fused into tube below. Stamens usually four, sometimes two to five. Stigma often two-lobed, ovary two-chambered, fruit a many-seeded capsule. Some scrophs with square stems and opposite leaves resemble mints, but lack mint aroma.

If there are bracts as long as or longer than flowers, sometimes brightly colored, go to

If bracts are shorter, or are missing, and flowers are:

- irregular, obviously two-lipped, go to next page.

- nearly regular, not two-lipped, go to page 114.

 If petals are easy to find, brightly colored, not green, go to page 108.

If petals are green, partly hidden by sepals and bracts, and bracts are:

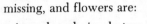

- magenta-pink, it is **Meadow Paintbrush** —
  Castilleia lemmonii

- greenish; flowers whitish, it is **Alpine Paintbrush** —
  C. nana

Other Sierra species with yellow, orange or red bracts include:
C. culbertsonii, C. breweri, C. applegatei, C. miniata, C. chromosa.

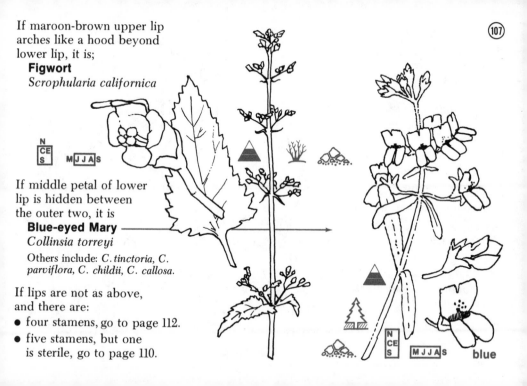

If maroon-brown upper lip arches like a hood beyond lower lip, it is;

Figwort
Scrophularia californica

If middle petal of lower lip is hidden between the outer two, it is

Blue-eyed Mary
Collinsia torreyi

Others include: *C. tinctoria, C. parviflora, C. childii, C. callosa.*

If lips are not as above, and there are:
- four stamens, go to page 112.
- five stamens, but one is sterile, go to page 110.

blue

If flowers are scattered;
petals with lower
lip white, it is
Pelican Flower ⟶
Cordylanthus tenuis
Other hard to tell
apart species occur.

If flowers are in dense racemes
or spikes, and have:

● sac-like (inflated) lower lips,
hooked upper lips, and are:

– white and purple, it is
Owl's Clover ⟶
Orthocarpus copelandii

– bright yellow, it is
Mountain Cream Sacs ⟶
O. lacerus

● hatchet-shaped or snout-
like upper lips,
go to next page.

If flowers are:

- dull yellow, it is
  Indian Warrior
  Pedicularis semibarbata

- purple, with long,
  snout-like upper
  lip, it is
  Elephant Snouts ———→
  P. groenlandica

  P. attolens, shorter
  with uncurled "snout"
  also occurs in Sierra.

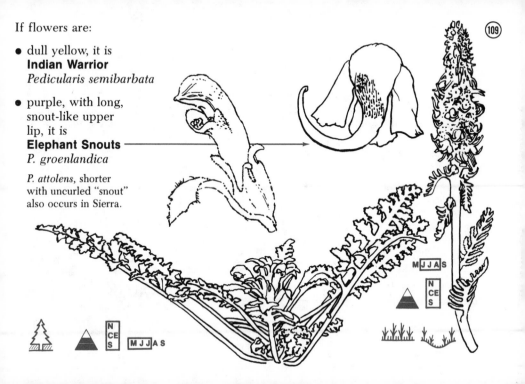

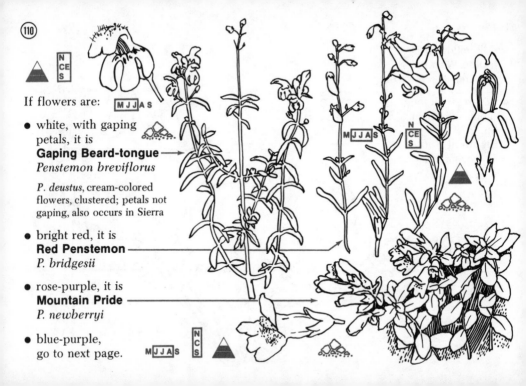

If flowers are:

- white, with gaping petals, it is **Gaping Beard-tongue** *Penstemon breviflorus* →

  P. deustus, cream-colored flowers, clustered; petals not gaping, also occurs in Sierra

- bright red, it is **Red Penstemon** → *P. bridgesii*

- rose-purple, it is **Mountain Pride** → *P. newberryi*

- blue-purple, go to next page.

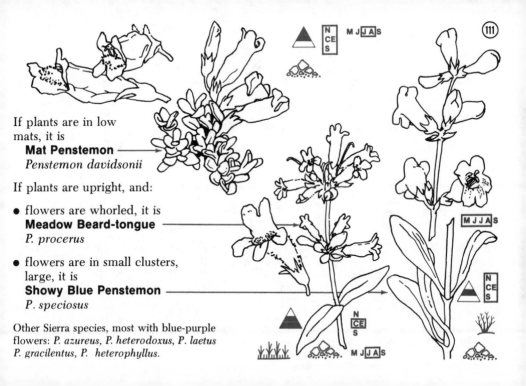

If plants are in low mats, it is
Mat Penstemon
Penstemon davidsonii

If plants are upright, and:

- flowers are whorled, it is
  Meadow Beard-tongue
  P. procerus

- flowers are in small clusters, large, it is
  Showy Blue Penstemon
  P. speciosus

Other Sierra species, most with blue-purple flowers: *P. azureus, P. heterodoxus, P. laetus P. gracilentus, P. heterophyllus.*

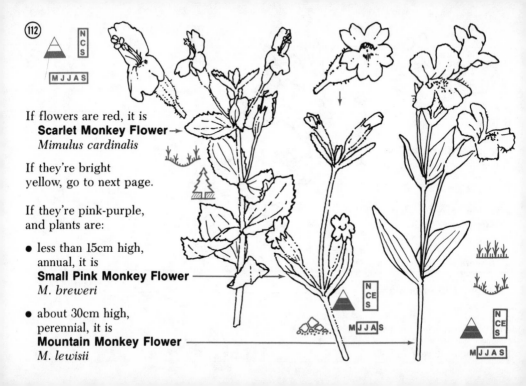

If flowers are red, it is
Scarlet Monkey Flower →
Mimulus cardinalis

If they're bright
yellow, go to next page.

If they're pink-purple,
and plants are:

- less than 15cm high,
  annual, it is
  Small Pink Monkey Flower →
  M. breweri

- about 30cm high,
  perennial, it is
  Mountain Monkey Flower →
  M. lewisii

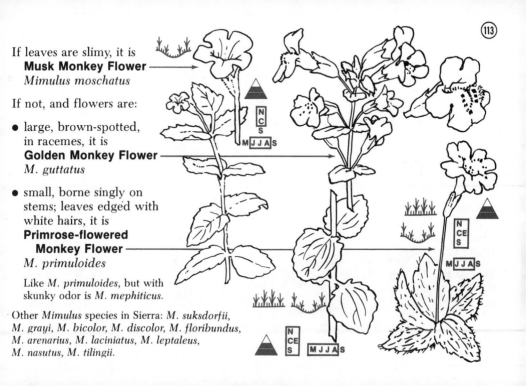

If leaves are slimy, it is
Musk Monkey Flower —————➤
Mimulus moschatus

If not, and flowers are:

- large, brown-spotted,
  in racemes, it is
  Golden Monkey Flower —————➤
  M. guttatus

- small, borne singly on
  stems; leaves edged with
  white hairs, it is
  Primrose-flowered
  Monkey Flower —————➤
  M. primuloides

  Like *M. primuloides*, but with
  skunky odor is *M. mephiticus.*

Other *Mimulus* species in Sierra: *M. suksdorfii,
M. grayi, M. bicolor, M. discolor, M. floribundus,
M. arenarius, M. laciniatus, M. leptaleus,
M. nasutus, M. tilingii.*

If flowers are blue-purple; stamens two; stems creeping, it is
Speedwell
American Brooklime
Veronica americana

Other Sierra species, most with upright stems, include: *V. alpina*, *V. serpyllifolia*, *V. peregrina*, *V. scutellata*.

If flowers are yellow; stamens five, it is
Common Mullein
Verbascum thapsus

Solanaceae (Tomato, Potato or Nightshade Family) Flowers have five partly fused sepals, five mostly fused petals, sometimes pleated in bud, also five stamens which sometimes stick together. Fruit a capsule or many-seeded berry.

One Sierra species: **Blue Witch**
Blue Nightshade
Solanum xantii

blue-purple

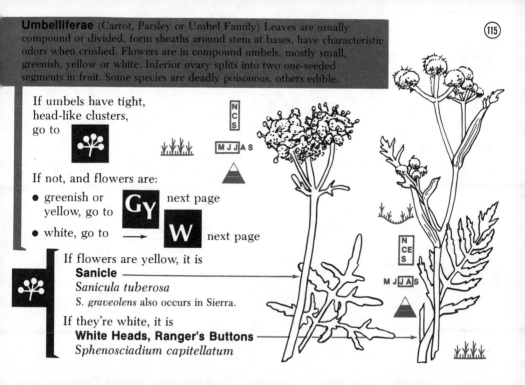

Umbelliferae (Carrot, Parsley or Umbel Family) Leaves are usually compound or divided, form sheaths around stem at bases, have characteristic odors when crushed. Flowers are in compound umbels, mostly small, greenish, yellow or white. Inferior ovary splits into two one-seeded segments in fruit. Some species are deadly poisonous, others edible.

If umbels have tight, head-like clusters, go to

If not, and flowers are:

● greenish or yellow, go to **G Y** next page

● white, go to → **W** next page

If flowers are yellow, it is
Sanicle
Sanicula tuberosa
S. *graveolens* also occurs in Sierra.

If they're white, it is
White Heads, Ranger's Buttons
Sphenosciadium capitellatum

G·Y

If flowers are greenish, foliage licorice-scented, it is
Sweet Cicely
Osmorhiza occidentalis
Also in Sierra: *O. chilensis*, *O. brachypoda*.

If flowers are yellow, go to **Y**

Y

If leaves are green, it is
Biscuit Root
Lomatium torreyi
Less common in Sierra: *L. nudicaule*, *L. nevadense* (white flowers).

If they're grey-green, it is *Pteryxia terebinthina*, not illustrated.

W

If plants are in or next to water, go to next page.

If not, and:
- leaves have few, coarse divisions, go to → p. 118
- leaves have several fine, often narrow divisions, go to → p. 118

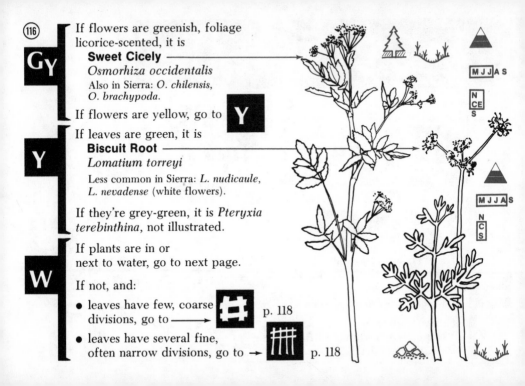

If leaves are divided several times, so that divisions have divisions, at least at their lower parts, it is
Water Hemlock
Cicuta douglasii

Water Hemlock is deadly poisonous. Upper roots are chambered inside.

If leaves are only once divided, and leaflets are:

● paired, 10 to 18, it is
Oxypolis
Oxypolis occidentalis

● not paired, of an odd number, 5 to 13, it is
Water Parsnip
Berula erecta

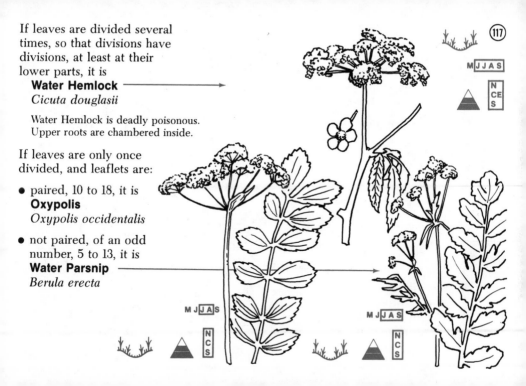

If leaves are divided into a few uneven, ragged segments; flowering stalks often over 1.3m tall, it is
Cow Parsnip
Heracleum lanatum

If leaves are divided into more than six symmetrical segments, it is
Angelica
Angelica breweri

A. lineariloba, very narrow, long leaflets, also occurs in Sierra.

If leaf divisions are widely separated; plants growing from tubers, it is Yampah. See next page.

If leaf divisions are broad, often in threes, it is
Mountain Lovage
Ligusticum grayi

(Also check Lomatium, p. 116.)

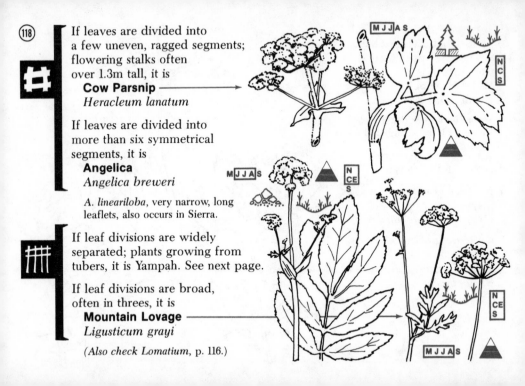

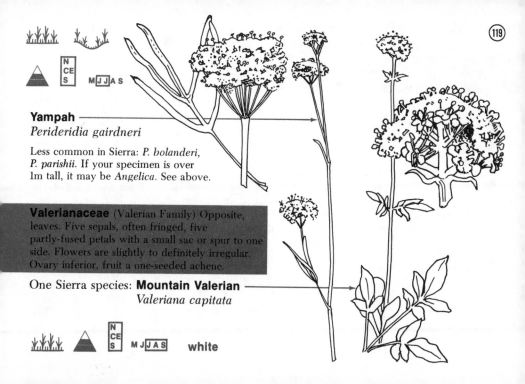

Yampah ——
Perideridia gairdneri

Less common in Sierra: *P. bolanderi*,
P. parishii. If your specimen is over
1m tall, it may be *Angelica*. See above.

Valerianaceae (Valerian Family) Opposite,
leaves. Five sepals, often fringed, five
partly-fused petals with a small sac or spur to one
side. Flowers are slightly to definitely irregular.
Ovary inferior, fruit a one-seeded achene.

One Sierra species: **Mountain Valerian** ——
Valeriana capitata

white

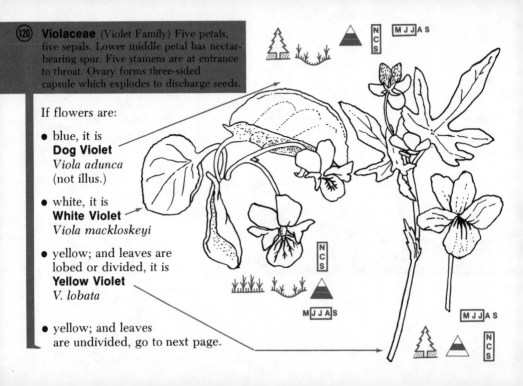

(120) **Violaceae** (Violet Family) Five petals, five sepals. Lower middle petal has nectar-bearing spur. Five stamens are at entrance to throat. Ovary forms three-sided capsule which explodes to discharge seeds.

If flowers are:

- blue, it is
  Dog Violet
  Viola adunca
  (not illus.)

- white, it is
  White Violet
  Viola mackloskeyi

- yellow; and leaves are lobed or divided, it is
  Yellow Violet
  V. lobata

- yellow; and leaves are undivided, go to next page.

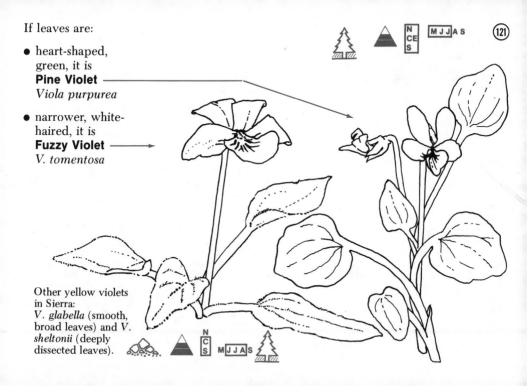

If leaves are:

- heart-shaped,
  green, it is
  Pine Violet
  Viola purpurea

- narrower, white-
  haired, it is
  Fuzzy Violet
  V. tomentosa

Other yellow violets
in Sierra:
V. glabella (smooth,
broad leaves) and *V.
sheltonii* (deeply
dissected leaves).

other books like this one, and what they identify

for North America east of the Rocky Mountains:

FLOWER FINDER — spring wildflowers and flower families
TREE FINDER — all native and introduced trees
WINTER TREE FINDER — leafless winter trees
FERN FINDER — native northeastern and midwestern ferns
TRACK FINDER — tracks and footprints of mammals
BERRY FINDER — native plants with fleshy fruits

for the Pacific coast states:

PACIFIC COAST TREE FINDER — native trees, Sitka to San Diego
PACIFIC COAST BIRD FINDER — 61 common birds
PACIFIC COAST BERRY FINDER — native plants with fleshy fruits
PACIFIC COAST FERN FINDER — native ferns and fern relatives
REDWOOD REGION FLOWER FINDER — wildflowers and families
SIERRA FLOWER FINDER — wildflowers of the Sierra Nevada
PACIFIC INTERTIDAL LIFE — organisms of tidepools, rocks, reefs

also:

DESERT TREE FINDER — trees of Arizona, California, New Mexico deserts
ROCKY MOUNTAIN TREE FINDER — native trees of Rocky Mountain area

for a catalog write NATURE STUDY GUILD
Box 972
Berkeley, California 94701